P9-CEJ-249

Eyewitness
SPACE
EXPLORATION

Hubble Space
Telescope

Potential damage
of space dust on
shuttle window

Satellite material

Japanese space agency
(NASDA) lapel pin

Toys taken into space

Patch worn by
first Mongolian
in space

Giotto space
probe

Spacesuit
designed for use
on the Moon

Residue
from solid
rocket boosters

Rock collected
on the Moon

Vase commemorating Polish
and Soviet space flight

Eyewitness
SPACE
EXPLORATION

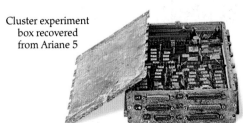

In-flight space clothes
worn on Mir

Written by
CAROLE STOTT

Photographed by
STEVE GORTON

Mir space station

Patch of Soviet
shuttle, Buran

Cluster experiment
box recovered
from Ariane 5

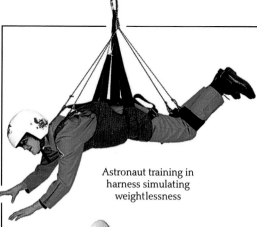

Astronaut training in
harness simulating
weightlessness

LONDON, NEW YORK, MELBOURNE, MUNICH, AND DELHI

Project editor Kitty Blount
Art editor Kati Poynor
Editor Julie Ferris
Managing editor Linda Martin
Managing art editor Julia Harris
Production Lisa Moss
Picture researcher Mo Sheerin
DTP designer Nicky Studdart

THIS EDITION
Editors Francesca Baines, Steve Setford
Art editors Catherine Goldsmith, Peter Radcliffe
Managing editor Jane Yorke
Managing art editors Owen Peyton Jones, Jane Thomas
Art director Martin Wilson
Associate publisher Andrew Macintyre
Picture researchers Harriet Mills, Sarah Pownall
Production editors Jenny Jacoby, Hitesh Patel
DTP designer Siu Yin Ho
Jacket editor Adam Powley
US editor Margaret Parrish

This Eyewitness ® Guide has been conceived by
Dorling Kindersley Limited and Editions Gallimard

First published in the United States in 1997
This revised edition published in the United States in 2002, 2010 by

DK Publishing
375 Hudson Street, New York, New York 10014

A catalog record for this book is
available from the Library of Congress.

ISBN 978-0-7566-5828-1

Color reproduction by Colourscan, Singapore; MDP, UK
Printed and bound by Toppan Printing Co., (Shenzhen) Ltd., China

Discover more at
www.dk.com

Telstar—transmitted first
live satellite television

Space food—
dehydrated fruit

Ariane 5 rocket

Patch worn by Sigmund Jahn, the first
astronaut of the German Democratic Republic

Progress craft carries supplies to
the International Space Station

Patch celebrating the first Indian
astronaut, Rakesh Sharma

Contents

Astronaut's footprint on
the lunar surface

Dreams of space

WINGED FLIGHT
In Greek mythology, Daedalus made a pair of wings for himself and his son Icarus in order to escape from a labyrinth. The wings were attached to their bodies with wax. But impetuous Icarus flew too close to the Sun, the wax melted, and he fell to Earth.

H<small>UMANS</small> <small>HAVE</small> <small>ALWAYS</small> <small>LOOKED</small> into the sky and wondered about what lies beyond Earth. For many, their curiosity stops there. Others dream of journeying into space, exploring the Moon, landing on Mars, or traveling to the stars. The dream of space travel and exploration turned to reality in the 20th century. The first practical steps were taken at the start of the century, as rockets were developed to blast away from Earth. In 1961, the first person reached space. By the end of the century, thousands of spacecraft and hundreds of space travelers had been launched into space. For many, the dream continues. A new generation of space travelers wants to go farther, stay longer, and learn more about space.

GOOSE TRAVEL
The Moon, Earth's closest neighbor, looms large in the sky. Light and dark areas on its surface are clearly visible. The apparent proximity of the Moon made it the object of many dream journeys into space. In a 17th-century story, wild geese took 11 days to carry a man to the Moon.

FACT MEETS FICTION
As humans learned more about their surroundings in space, the stories of space travel became more realistic. In the late 19th century, the French author Jules Verne wrote stories using fact as well as science fiction. His characters journeyed to the Moon in a shell fired by a giant cannon.

SKY WATCHING
Our present knowledge of space is built partly on information learned by the sky watchers of ancient civilizations. Thousands of years ago, basic distances were established and the regular movements of the Sun, Moon, and planets were used for timekeeping and to understand how Earth fit into the universe.

SPACE MONEY
This Moscow statue of a rocket being launched is a mark of the importance Russia placed on its astronauts and space exploration. In the 1940s and 1950s, research into space travel had been developed by national governments and began to receive serious financial backing. Policies for space travel and exploration and strategies for using space were established.

MUSIC OF SPACE
Space and its contents—the Moon, planets, and stars—have inspired story writers, poets, and musicians. In 1916, Gustav Holst, a Swedish composer, completed an orchestral suite called "The Planets." As the space race was gathering momentum, the American singer Frank Sinatra (left) was performing love ballads, including "Fly Me to the Moon." And the Moon has often been depicted as a magical land in rhymes and stories for children.

TELESCOPE POWER
Until the 17th century, people believed that the Sun, Moon, planets, and stars all revolved around the Earth. Observations made by Galileo Galilei, an Italian astronomer, through the newly invented telescope, revealed that space contained far more than had been thought, and helped show that Earth—and thus, humankind—was not at its center.

SPACE ROCK

Space made an appearance in popular culture in the 1960s and 1970s, when fashion and music showed the influence of the space age. David Bowie (right) took on the persona of spaceman Ziggy Stardust, and his songs "Space Oddity" and "Is There Life on Mars?" echoed the concerns of the space scientists.

COMIC CAPERS

The dream of space was at its wildest in the comics of the 1930s through to the 1950s. Authors and artists let their imaginations run riot. Aliens were featured regularly, from encounters in space to landings on Everest. But many other stories were not so far-fetched and only heralded space ventures that were to become reality within decades.

Exploring the Moon would soon become a reality

JOIN TOGETHER

Individuals dreaming of space travel join together to form societies. The first was established in Germany in 1927, followed by others in the US and Britain. A leading figure in the British society was Arthur C. Clarke, whose ideas helped to influence space research. His articles and books deal with science fiction as well as science fact. He foresaw the use of satellites for communicating globally and showed us the space future in his books and articles, and also in the innovative film *2001: A Space Odyssey*.

Earth seen from the Moon

Cratered lunar surface

Astronaut holding the US flag

20TH-CENTURY ICON

In 1986, medieval figures that had adorned the roof of Britain's York Minster Cathedral were destroyed in a fire. They were replaced by this potent symbol of the 20th century—humankind conquering space. For hundreds of years to come, worshiping Christians will gaze up at this icon of our times.

SPACE HERO AND HEROINE

Today's children were born into the space age and know that space exploration is a reality. They understand how a satellite works, they know what space is like, and they look forward to exploring it. Even young children's toy hero Action Man (right) and heroine Barbie (above) have apparently both been to space!

What is space?

SURROUNDING EARTH IS A BLANKET OF AIR, its atmosphere. It both provides the oxygen we need to stay alive and protects us from the heat of the Sun in the day, and from the cold, sunless night. Away from Earth's surface, the air thins and its composition and temperature change. These changes continue as the altitude increases. The transition from Earth's atmosphere to space is gradual—there is no obvious barrier to cross. Above about 600 miles (1,000 km) from Earth is space, but many conditions associated with space are experienced within a few hundred miles of Earth, where satellites and astronauts work. Astronauts are said to be in space once they reach 60 miles (100 km) above Earth.

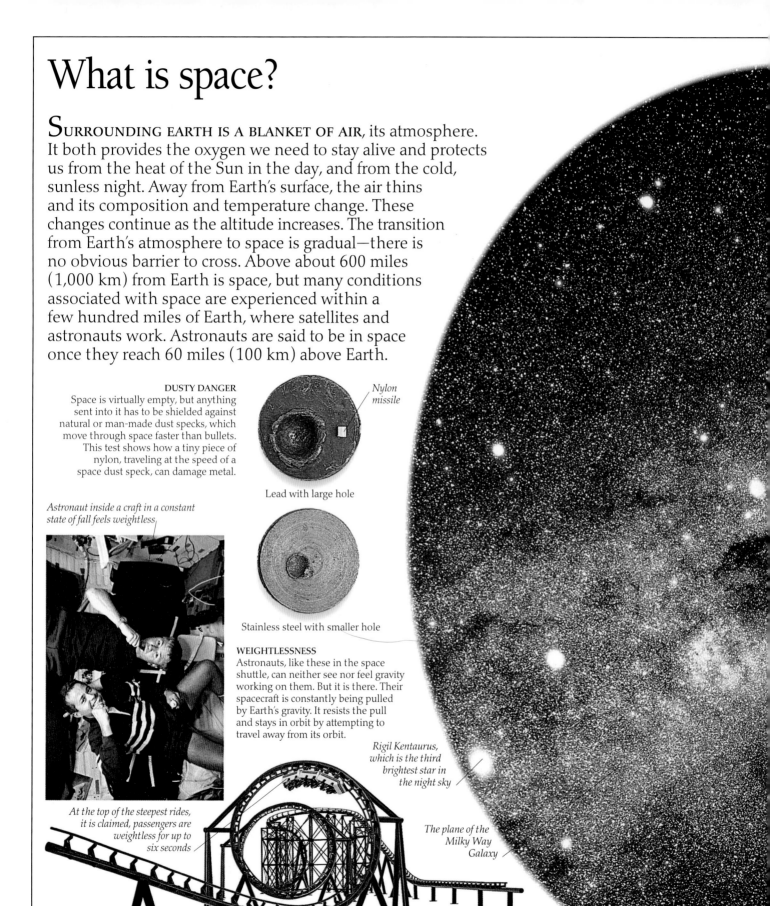

DUSTY DANGER
Space is virtually empty, but anything sent into it has to be shielded against natural or man-made dust specks, which move through space faster than bullets. This test shows how a tiny piece of nylon, traveling at the speed of a space dust speck, can damage metal.

Nylon missile

Lead with large hole

Stainless steel with smaller hole

Astronaut inside a craft in a constant state of fall feels weightless

WEIGHTLESSNESS
Astronauts, like these in the space shuttle, can neither see nor feel gravity working on them. But it is there. Their spacecraft is constantly being pulled by Earth's gravity. It resists the pull and stays in orbit by attempting to travel away from its orbit.

Rigil Kentaurus, which is the third brightest star in the night sky

At the top of the steepest rides, it is claimed, passengers are weightless for up to six seconds

The plane of the Milky Way Galaxy

ROLLER COASTER
As a car goes over a hump in the road, the passengers' stomachs fall slightly after their body frames. They momentarily experience weightlessness. A roller coaster ride has a more dramatic effect, and the feeling can last for a few seconds. Modified aircraft give astronauts the chance to train in weightlessness for about 25 seconds.

LOOKING INTO SPACE

When we look at the night sky, we can see tens of thousands of stars, which, like the Sun, our own star, belong to the Milky Way Galaxy, partly shown here. Beyond are more than 100 billion, billion stars in other galaxies, which, along with trillions of miles of virtually empty space, make up the rest of the universe. We have explored space only within the solar system, made up of the Sun and the planets that orbit around it.

HUMANS IN SPACE

Most astronauts, like these, have traveled into space close to Earth, where they use the planet's gravity to orbit around it. Only 26 have traveled farther, to the Moon. Wherever humans go in space, they need to take their own atmosphere and protection against the new environment.

Suits protect astronauts from temperatures ranging from 250°F (121°C) to −150°F (−101°C)

Rock from Mars fell to Earth about 13,000 years ago

Voyager spacecraft is prepared for launch in 1977

DOWN TO EARTH

Scientists get the chance to study space material by sending robotic craft, or astronauts, to investigate it on site, or bring it back to Earth. They also study chunks of it that have found their own way here. Every year, over 3,000 bits of space rock fall to Earth. Most land in the sea, but a handful are collected.

MESSAGE FROM EARTH

It is believed that 1 in every 25 stars has planets. The Sun has eight, and since 1992 more than 340 have been discovered orbiting other stars. Of these, Earth is the only planet known to have life. However, some spacecraft, such as Voyager, carry messages in case intelligent life does exist elsewhere.

Disc with message

Earth's highest mountain, Everest, is 29,029 ft (8,848 m) above sea level

HIGH ALTITUDE EXPLORERS

There is no need to leave Earth to experience a change in altitude and a consequent change in the Earth's atmosphere. Mountaineers know that the air gets thinner the higher they climb. At around 12,000 ft (3,700 m), there is less oxygen, and they need to carry their own. High-altitude balloonists travel in pressurized cabins. At about 12 miles (19 km) above sea level, atmospheric pressure is so low that body fluids vaporize and force their way through membranes, such as eyes and mouths.

Space nations

PEOPLE FROM AROUND THE WORLD are involved in space exploration. The vast majority will never go anywhere near space, but it is a major part of their lives. Fewer than 10 of the world's countries regularly launch vehicles into space, but many more countries are involved in the preparation and manufacture of spacecraft and technology. Others are involved in monitoring space activities, or in simply reaping the benefits of space exploration—from the knowledge they gain of the universe, to the cheap and instant telephone calls they make via satellites. Some nations work alone, others pool financial resources, knowledge, and expertise. Sending an astronaut, a space probe, or a satellite into space is a billion-dollar venture, which is achieved by thousands of people, and which benefits hundreds of thousands more.

MISSION PATCH
Space missions, both manned and unmanned, have emblems that are often made into cloth patches measuring a couple of inches across. They feature a selection of pictures and words representing the mission. France was the first nation to have astronauts fly aboard Soviet and United States (US) spacecraft. Jean-Loup Chretien's stay aboard Salyut 7 in 1982 was marked by this patch.

Engine nozzle

Thruster rockets for fine control

UNITED STATES

APOLLO 18
The US's Apollo 18 completed the first international space rendezvous when it maneuvered toward the Soviet Soyuz 19 in 1975. It carried the docking adaptor to join the two craft.

GETTING THERE
Metals and parts used in spacecraft are produced by many manufacturers and brought together for assembly and testing. The completed craft is then transported to the launch site. A large piece of space equipment, such as this major part of the Ariane 5 rocket, is transported by water. Here, it is being pulled through a harbor on route to its launch site at Kourou in French Guiana, South America.

КОСМОС ДЛЯ МИРА
COSMOS FOR PEACE

MISSION CONTROL, CHINA
China sent its first satellite Mao 1 into space in 1970. It became the third nation to launch a human when its first taikonaut (Chinese astronaut) entered space in October 2003. This picture shows mission control staff at the Xichang site practicing launch procedure.

SOUNDS OF SPACE
Space exploration has inspired people around the world to paint, write, and compose. This two-disc recording was released in 1975 at the time of the Apollo-Soyuz docking as a celebration of Soviet space achievement. One disc includes space-to-ground transmission. The second plays patriotic songs. One song is sung by Yuri Gagarin, who was the first man ever to go into space.

Giant dish provides telephone and television links

THE EARS OF THE WORLD
Ground stations around the world are listening in to space. Giant dishes collect data transmitted by distant planetary probes, satellite observatories looking into space and monitoring Earth, and communications satellites providing telephone links and television pictures. This 39 ft 4 in (12 m) dish at Lhasa in Tibet is used for telecommunications.

INDIA IN SPACE
India launched its first satellite in 1980, becoming the seventh nation to launch a space rocket. This patch marks the flight of Indian astronaut Rakesh Sharma to the Salyut 7 space station in April 1984.

HEADLINE NEWS
Sending astronauts into space has become such a regular event that it is reported on the inside pages of a newspaper, if at all. But when a country's first astronaut is launched, it makes headline news. The flights of the first astronaut from Poland, Miroslaw Hermaszewski, in 1978, and of the first Cuban astronaut, Arnaldo Tamayo Mendez, in 1980, were celebrated in their national press.

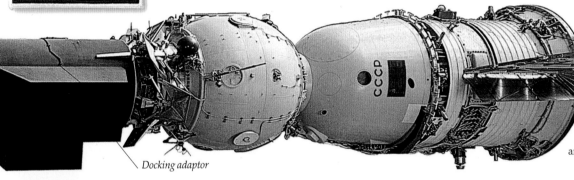

Docking adaptor

SOYUZ 19
Soyuz 19 was launched first, from the Soviet Union, a few hours before Apollo 18 left the US. During docking, Soyuz kept pointing at Apollo and rolled to match its movement.

INTERNATIONAL RENDEZVOUS
In 1975, Americans and Soviets linked up for the first time in space. Three US astronauts aboard Apollo 18, and two Soviets on Soyuz 19, flew in tandem as they orbited the world. Once docked on July 17, they stayed together for two days. Since the 1990s, the Americans and Russians have worked together regularly in space, first on Mir, and later on the International Space Station (ISS).

Aleksei Leonov (center) with Americans Thomas Stafford and Donald Slayton

WELCOME GIFT
International space crews exchange gifts. Russians sometimes give candies like these. Space crew aboard Mir greeted visiting astronauts with a traditional Russian gift of bread and salt as the visitors entered the space station. On Earth, the white floury bread is broken and eaten after dipping it in roughly cut salt. The food had been adapted into prepackaged bread and salt wafers for space travel.

Prunariu's mission patch, showing the flag of Romania

Gurragcha's mission patch, showing the flag of Mongolia

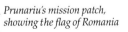

ROMANIA IN SPACE
Dumitru Prunariu was the first Romanian to enter space when he flew on Soyuz 40 to the Salyut 6 space station in May 1981. Along with Soviet astronaut Leonid Popov, Prunariu underwent psychological and medical tests. The custom of photographing the visiting astronaut's country was carried out as the station passed over Romania in daylight.

SEARCHING MONGOLIA
The eighth international crew on board a Soviet space station included Mongolian astronaut Jugderdemidiyn Gurragcha, who was on board Salyut 6 for eight days in March 1981. He performed a number of experiments. Using mapping and other cameras, he searched for possible ore and petroleum deposits in Mongolia.

Rocket science

A ROCKET IS NEEDED to launch anything and anyone into space. It provides the power to lift itself and its cargo off the ground and, in a short space of time, the power to attain the speed that will carry it away from gravity's pull and into space. The burning rocket fuels produce hot gases that are expelled through an exhaust nozzle at the bottom of the rocket. This provides the force that lifts the vehicle off the ground. The space rocket was developed in the first half of the 20th century. Typically two rockets a week are launched into space from somewhere in the world.

EARLY ROCKETS
The earliest rockets were used by the Chinese about a thousand years ago. They were powered by gunpowder. Once ignited, an explosive burst propelled the rocket forward. They resembled firework rockets but were used as weapons. This 17th-century man shot rocket arrows from a basket.

ROCKET PIONEER
Konstantin Tsiolkovsky, a Russian, started working on the theory of rocket space flight in the 1880s. He figured out how fast a rocket needed to go and how much fuel it would require. He proposed using liquid fuel, and using fuel in several stages.

ROCKET ENGINE
This is just one of four Viking engines that powered the Ariane 1 rocket—seen from below as it stands on the launch pad. In under two and a half minutes, and 31 miles (50 km) above the launch pad, its job was over.

Giant Viking rocket engine

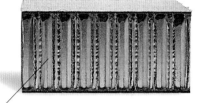

Honeycomb material is light and strong

Honeycomb structure is visible from the top

MADE TO MEASURE
The materials used in rockets and their cargoes need to be light. This is because a lighter rocket needs less fuel to launch it, and so it is less costly. The materials also need to be strong and able to withstand the thrust at launch. Some widely available materials, such as steel, are used. Others, like this honeycomb material, are specially developed and manufactured by rocket scientists and space engineers.

Nozzle where gases produced by burning fuel in the booster rocket are expelled

Pipe delivers oxygen to hydrogen for combustion

Flags of nations involved in the Ariane 5 project

28 tons (25 metric tons) of liquid hydrogen stored in tank

Solid rocket boosters supply 90 percent of thrust at liftoff

143 tons (130 metric tons) liquid oxygen in separate tank

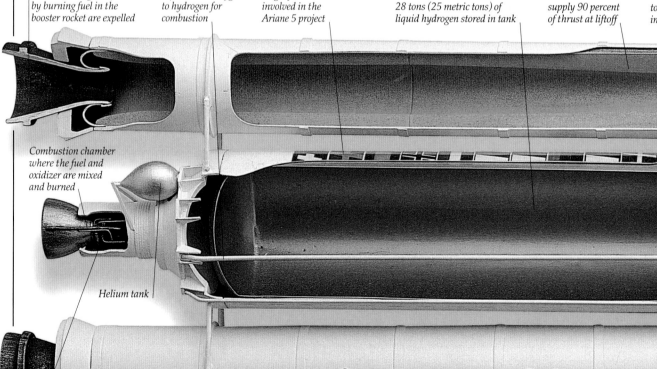

Combustion chamber where the fuel and oxidizer are mixed and burned

Helium tank

Liftoff procedure starts with the ignition of this Vulcain engine

French Space Agency emblem

Two boosters are ignited before the main rocket to supply initial thrust

European Space Agency (ESA) emblem

French rocket-manufacturing company (Arianespace) emblem

LIQUID-FUEL ROCKET
American Robert Goddard was fascinated by the idea of space travel. He experimented with rockets and different fuels. He launched the first-ever liquid-fuel rocket in 1926. The flight lasted two and a half seconds and the rocket reached an altitude of 41 ft (12.5 m).

ROCKET CAR
Fuel for use in rockets was tested in cars, rail vehicles, air gliders, and ice sleds in the 1920s. The cars resembled a rocket in shape and in the noise they made as they used the fuel. They used either liquid fuel or powdered solid fuel. The men who built and drove the cars were members of the newly formed German Society for Space Travel.

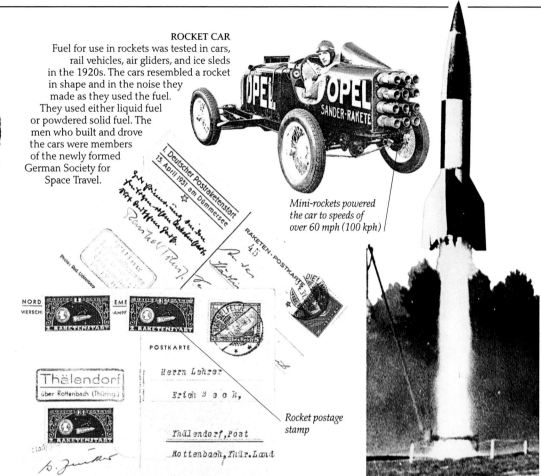

Mini-rockets powered the car to speeds of over 60 mph (100 kph)

ROCKET MAIL
Enterprising ways of using rocket power were developed in the 1930s. These cards were sent across Germany by rocket mail in 1931. They were specially produced cards, using special rocket postage stamps. Ventures such as this one were short-lived.

Rocket postage stamp

FIRST TO SPACE
The V2 rocket was developed in Germany in the 1930s. Its first successful launch was in 1942, and it became the first mass-produced long-range rocket. It was first used as a weapon. Over 4,000 were fired in the last year of World War II against Britain. After the war, the V2 and subsequent rockets for space travel were developed by an American team headed by Wernher von Braun.

ISLAND TO SPACE
Japan's Tanegashima Space Center is one of about 30 launch sites around the world where rockets start their space journeys. From this island site, the Japanese Space Agency assembles, tests, launches, and keeps track of satellites. Japan became the fourth nation into space when it launched its first satellite in 1970. Launch sites are built close to the equator to benefit from an extra push from Earth's spin at launch.

Parachute in nose cone for slow descent

Engine and fuel to move the pair of satellites into the correct orbit

Up to four satellites, like this one, can be carried into space

ARIANE 5
The Ariane rocket is the launch vehicle of the European Space Agency (ESA). The agency is made up of 18 European countries that fund and develop craft and experiments for space. Over 170 satellites have been launched by the Ariane rocket from the ESA launch site at Kourou in French Guiana. The latest of the Ariane series, Ariane 5, is the most powerful. It is therefore able to launch heavy single satellites, or a few smaller ones. Its initial design included room for astronauts to be transported in a specially modified upper stage.

Reusable rocket

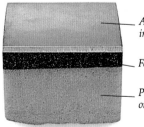

PIGGYBACK
When a shuttle orbiter (space plane) needs to be moved to a launch site, it is transported piggyback style on top of a specially adapted Boeing 747 aircraft. The orbiter's rocket motors are protected by an aerodynamic tail-cover. The shuttle is then prepared for launch and is equipped with boosters and fuel tank for liftoff.

WHEN THE FIRST SPACE SHUTTLE was launched in 1981, it marked a turning point in space travel. Conventional one-use rockets had until then been the only way of sending astronauts or cargoes into space. For regular space travel, a reusable system was needed. The United States came up with the answer in the form of the Space Transportation System (STS), or shuttle, for short. Launched like a conventional rocket, it returns to Earth like a plane. This means that two of its three main parts are used over and over again. Shuttles transport crew and equipment to the International Space Station (ISS), launch, retrieve, and repair satellites, launch space probes, and are used as space laboratories. A new spacecraft, Orion (p. 58), is due to take over the shuttle's duties in 2014.

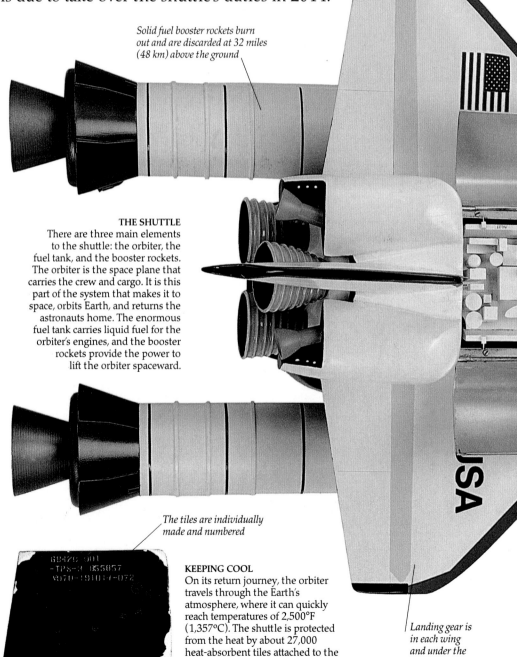

Solid fuel booster rockets burn out and are discarded at 32 miles (48 km) above the ground

THE SHUTTLE
There are three main elements to the shuttle: the orbiter, the fuel tank, and the booster rockets. The orbiter is the space plane that carries the crew and cargo. It is this part of the system that makes it to space, orbits Earth, and returns the astronauts home. The enormous fuel tank carries liquid fuel for the orbiter's engines, and the booster rockets provide the power to lift the orbiter spaceward.

BLASTOFF
Within two minutes of the shuttle lifting off from the launch pad, the booster rockets are discarded, as is the fuel tank six minutes later. From liftoff to space takes less than 10 minutes. Since the first launch in 1981, there have been over 130 successful flights. Atlantis's launch, shown here, in October 1985 marked the start of the 21st shuttle mission.

Aluminum inner structure

Foam coating

Protective outer layer

SAFE INSIDE
The shuttle's aluminum fuel tank is higher than a 15-story building. It has been specially designed to carry and protect its cargo. Inside its outer layer, shown here, are two pressurized tanks that contain liquid hydrogen and liquid oxygen. During launch, the fuel is fed to the orbiter's three main engines.

The tiles are individually made and numbered

68429 001
-TPS-3 155857
V070-191014-072

KEEPING COOL
On its return journey, the orbiter travels through the Earth's atmosphere, where it can quickly reach temperatures of 2,500°F (1,357°C). The shuttle is protected from the heat by about 27,000 heat-absorbent tiles attached to the outside and a reinforced carbon compound on the nose and wings.

Landing gear is in each wing and under the orbiter's nose

SOVIET SHUTTLE
Other countries have researched and developed the principle of reusable space transportation, but only the Soviet Union has come close. November 1988 saw the only launch of the Soviet shuttle Buran. The crewless shuttle flew two orbits of Earth and returned by automatic landing.

HYPERSONIC AIRCRAFT
During the 1960s, the X-15 rocket-powered aircraft was used to investigate flight at hypersonic speeds. It was released at high altitude, where the rocket motors were ignited. The pilot controlled the X-15 at about 4,000 mph (6,500 kph). Experience gained with this craft was used in the design of the shuttle.

On board is Sally Ride, the first US female astronaut

SHUTTLE ASTRONAUTS
Each shuttle has a commander responsible for the whole flight, a pilot to help fly the orbiter, and a number of astronaut specialists. Mission specialists are in charge of the orbiter's systems and perform space walks. Payload specialists, who are not necessarily regular astronauts, work with particular equipment or experiments on board.

ORBITER IN FLIGHT
There are currently three orbiters in the US space shuttle fleet—Discovery, Atlantis, and Endeavour. Challenger, shown here, flew nine times before exploding after liftoff in 1986. Columbia disintegrated in 2003 as it returned to Earth on completion of its 28th flight.

Commander John Young (left) and pilot Robert Crippen in training for the first-ever shuttle flight

Payload bay doors open in orbit

Tunnel to Spacelab

Flight deck and crew quarters for up to eight astronauts

External fuel tank is emptied in the first eight and a half minutes of flight. It is discarded and breaks up in the atmosphere

Spacelab

Ockels in his slippers

Parachute helps the orbiter decelerate on the runway

Booster rockets fall safely into the ocean, where they are retrieved for reuse

INSIDE SPACELAB
Wubbo Ockels, a Dutch astronaut, was a payload specialist on Challenger's third mission in 1985. He worked in Spacelab (p. 36) during the seven-day flight. There were 75 experiments on board, several of which were designed to give scientists data on how space travel affects the human body (pp. 26–27).

SHUTTLE LANDING
An orbiter's onboard motors are used to maneuver it in space and to position it ready to come out of orbit and decelerate. The orbiter enters the atmosphere at 15,000 mph (24,000 kph), slowing all the time. A loss of communications then follows for 12 to 16 minutes. Then the orbiter touches down on the runway at 215 mph (344 kph), coming to rest after 1.5 miles (2.4 km).

The race for space

TWO NATIONS DOMINATED one of the most intense and successful periods of space exploration. For around 15 years, centered on the 1960s, the United States and the Soviet Union raced against each other to achieve success in space. Each wanted to make notable firsts: to be the first to put a satellite, and then a man, into space; to have the first astronaut in orbit and the first woman space traveler; to make the first space walk outside a craft; and to be the first to step on the Moon. The race got under way when the Soviets launched Sputnik 1, proving their space capability to the surprised Americans. From then on, each leapt forward in turn as new space achievements were made one after another.

UNITED CIGARETTES
These cigarettes celebrate the docking of the US craft Apollo 18 and the Soviet Soyuz 19 in space in July 1975.

Apollo-Soyuz union cigarettes were printed in English on one side and Russian on the other

Aluminum sphere 1 ft 11 in (58 cm) across with four antennae

SPUTNIK 1
The space age started on October 4, 1957, when the first artificial satellite was launched by the Soviets. The satellite helped scientists learn more about the nature of Earth's uppermost atmosphere. As it orbited Earth every 96 minutes, its two radio transmitters signaled "bleep, bleep."

EXPLORER 1
Vanguard, the rocket that was to carry the first US satellite into space, exploded on the launch pad. However, the satellite, Explorer 1, was already being constructed and, on January 31, 1958, it became the first American satellite in space. The Van Allen radiation belts surrounding Earth were discovered using scientific equipment on board.

Explorer 1 orbited Earth for 12 years

Service module was jettisoned before reentry into Earth's atmosphere

Electrodes were attached to Laika to monitor her heart and breathing

Luna 3 transmitted the first views of the far side of the Moon

LUNA 3
In 1959, the first of the Luna series of craft was launched by the Soviets. Luna 1 was the first spacecraft to leave Earth's gravity. Luna 9 was the first craft to make a successful landing on the Moon. The Soviets also sent the first of their Venera series to Venus in 1961.

FIRST CREATURE TO ORBIT EARTH
Only one month after the launch of Sputnik 1, the Soviets launched the first creature into orbit around Earth, aboard Sputnik 2. A dog named Laika traveled in a padded pressurized compartment and survived for a few days. The satellite was much heavier than anything the US was planning and suggested the Soviets were considering putting humans into orbit. American pride was injured and space became a political issue. The United States resolved to enter and win the race.

APOLLO 11
In the early 1960s, 377,000 Americans worked to get a man on the Moon. Ten Gemini two-manned missions successfully showed that the Americans could spacewalk, spend time in space, and dock craft. These were all necessary for the next three-manned Apollo program, the one that would take men to the Moon (pp. 20–21).

FIRST AMONG EQUALS
Yuri Gagarin became the first human in space on April 12, 1961. Strapped in his Vostok 1 capsule, he orbited Earth once before reentering Earth's atmosphere. After 108 minutes in space, he ejected himself from the capsule and parachuted to Earth. With him here is Valentina Tereshkova, the first woman in space.

HERO'S WELCOME
Gagarin's countrymen turned out in force to welcome him home from space. They filled the enormous Red Square in the heart of Moscow. But Gagarin was not only a hero in the Soviet Union. In the months ahead, crowds turned out to greet him wherever he toured.

Three-manned crew worked and slept in the command module, the only part of the mission to return to Earth

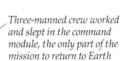

A PRESIDENT'S PROMISE
In the late 1950s, the US increased space research funding and formed a space agency, the National Aeronautics and Space Administration (NASA). Its first goal was to place a man in space. The Soviets beat the US to it by one month. But in May 1961, the new US president, John F. Kennedy, set a new goal of "landing a man on the Moon and returning him safely to the Earth" before the decade was out.

FIRST SPACE WALK
Once humans had successfully flown into space, both the Soviets and the Americans prepared to let them move outside their craft in space. The first extra-vehicular activity (EVA), or space walk, was made by Soviet Aleksei Leonov in March 1965. He spent 10 minutes in space secured to his Voskhod 2 craft.

Command and service modules, where crew is located

LIFTOFF
The US's Saturn V rocket was developed to launch the Apollo craft to the Moon. As tall as a 30-story building, it was the most powerful rocket to date. The majority of its bulk was fuel. The top third of the rocket consisted of the lunar module for landing on the Moon; the service module providing the oxygen, water, and power for the crew; and, right on top, the command module.

THE MOON TO MEXICO
Michael Collins (left), Buzz Aldrin (rear), and Neil Armstrong (right) of Apollo 11, the first mission to land a man on the Moon, are greeted in Mexico City. The three visited 24 countries in 45 days as part of a goodwill tour after their safe return from the Moon. One million people had turned up in Florida to see the start of their journey, but many more welcomed them home. Collins orbited the Moon in the command module, while the others explored the lunar surface.

Space travelers

AROUND 500 PEOPLE and countless other living creatures have traveled from Earth into space. All but 26 of them, men who went to the Moon, have spent their time in space in a craft orbiting Earth. Competition to travel into space is keen. When a call for potential European astronauts was made in June 2008, more than 8,400 people applied. Astronauts are men and women with an outstanding ability in a scientific discipline, who are both mentally and physically fit. Originally, animals went into space to test the conditions prior to the first human flight. Now, along with insects and other creatures, they accompany astronauts and are used for scientific research.

Symbol of the International Aeronautical Federation

Passport requests, in five languages, that any necessary help be given to the holder

Photograph of Helen Sharman, British astronaut and owner of this passport

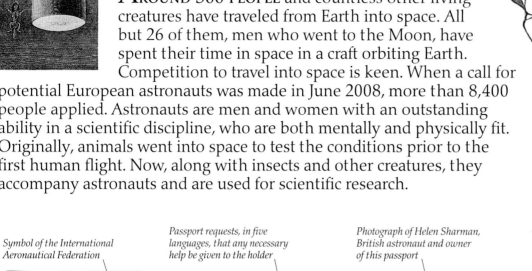

№ 087

PASSPORT TO SPACE
Astronauts can carry a passport for space travel in case it is needed when they return to Earth. An unscheduled landing may be made in a country other than that of the launch. The type shown here is carried by astronauts on Russian craft. The term astronaut describes space travelers from all countries. But those on board Russian craft are also called cosmonauts, and Chinese travelers are taikonauts.

UNTETHERED FLIGHT
Astronauts venturing outside a spacecraft must be tethered to the craft, or fixed to a moveable robotic arm, otherwise they will follow their own orbit around Earth. Used in 1984, the manned maneuvering unit (MMU) was a powered backpack that let the astronauts move freely in space.

American Bruce McCandless makes first space walk using a hand-controlled MMU, in 1984

Ham, the first chimpanzee astronaut

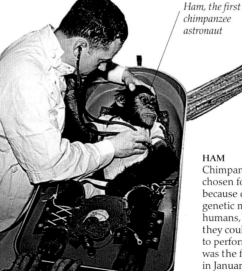

Belka

Strelka

HAM
Chimpanzees were chosen for space travel because of their similar genetic makeup to humans, and because they could be trained to perform tasks. Ham was the first to travel in January 1961. On his return, he was examined and found to be in excellent condition.

STRELKA AND BELKA
The Soviets launched a number of four-legged astronauts into space. The first to orbit Earth was the dog Laika, in 1957 (pp. 16–17). She perished in flight, but two other dogs, Strelka and Belka, returned safely to Earth by parachute in August 1960.

HONEYBEES
In April 1984, a comb of honeybees traveled aboard the space shuttle Challenger. Like most travelers into space, the bees found weightlessness confusing to start with. But, once they had acclimatized to life in space, they built their hive as successfully as they do on Earth.

Frog is placed in capsule for flight

SPINNING FROGS
Over 30 years ago, two bullfrogs orbited Earth to help medical research into the workings of the human inner ear. The frogs were monitored over a five-day period in both weightless and partial-gravity conditions. The frogs were spun in their capsule to create the partial gravity.

SQUIRREL MONKEY
The first monkey into space was a squirrel monkey, Gordo, in December 1958. Since then, dogs, monkeys, flies, fish, ants, frogs, sea urchins, and over 2,000 jellyfish have been some of the creatures to travel into space. They have been used for research into various subjects, including the effects of weightlessness, fertility, and reproduction.

Animal and human crews have backups, reserves in case one of the original crew becomes sick. This monkey backup is drinking some juice

Breathing mask provided oxygen

Hector, a white rat, was launched from France

READY FOR SPACE
Early animal travelers wore their own spacesuits. Several suits were tested by the Soviets to see which would give their astronaut dogs the most protection. Dogs were chosen because their blood circulation and respiration are close to our own, and they are patient creatures.

WHITE RAT
Mice and rats have traveled into space for about 50 years. One of the first, Hector, a white rat, soared 100 miles (160 km) into space in 1961, and landed safely back on Earth three minutes later, alive and well.

SPACE ZOO
Two monkeys, snails, beetles, and fruit midges traveled together in December 1996. After a two-week trip into space, they were tested for the effects of weightlessness before returning to their Earth zoo. They were loaded on board the Vostok rocket in their own capsule. Bone tissue from the monkeys' hip bones, taken before and after the flight, was used for medical research. Monkeys going into space were named in Russian alphabetical order. The winners of a school competition named these two Lapik and Multik.

Man on the Moon

THE MOON IS THE ONLY WORLD that humans have landed on outside their own. For centuries, Earth's companion in space aroused our interest and, as Earth's nearest neighbor, it was the most likely target for manned space travel. Twelve US astronauts touched down on the Moon between 1969 and 1972. They traveled in six separate Apollo missions and spent just over 300 hours on the Moon's surface—80 hours of that outside the landing craft. They collected rock samples, took photographs, and set up experiments to monitor the Moon's environment. The Apollo missions were followed worldwide.

Apollo 16 lunar module, code-named Orion

Upper part of Orion, which is where the astronauts lived while on the Moon, rejoined the command module for the return journey

Landing platform remained behind when Orion blasted off the Moon for the start of the return journey to Earth

Lunar module is shown from behind—entrance was on the other side

US flag needed a small telescopic arm to keep it extended on the airless Moon

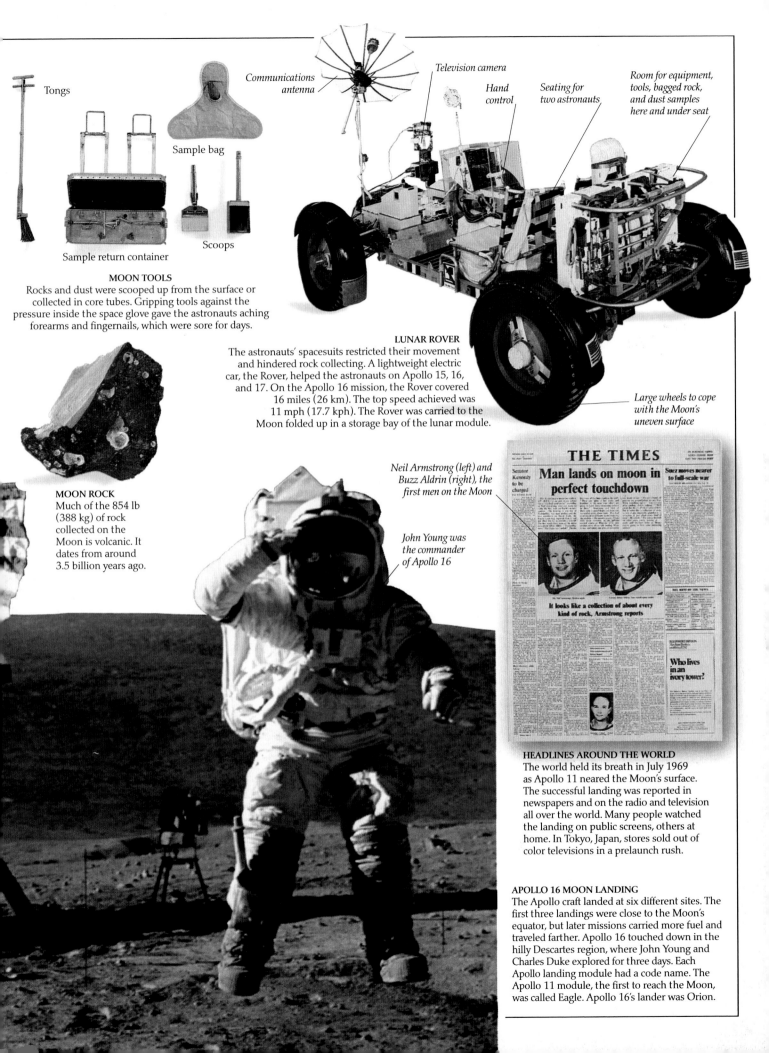

Tongs

Sample bag

Scoops

Sample return container

Communications antenna

Television camera

Hand control

Seating for two astronauts

Room for equipment, tools, bagged rock, and dust samples here and under seat

MOON TOOLS
Rocks and dust were scooped up from the surface or collected in core tubes. Gripping tools against the pressure inside the space glove gave the astronauts aching forearms and fingernails, which were sore for days.

LUNAR ROVER
The astronauts' spacesuits restricted their movement and hindered rock collecting. A lightweight electric car, the Rover, helped the astronauts on Apollo 15, 16, and 17. On the Apollo 16 mission, the Rover covered 16 miles (26 km). The top speed achieved was 11 mph (17.7 kph). The Rover was carried to the Moon folded up in a storage bay of the lunar module.

Large wheels to cope with the Moon's uneven surface

MOON ROCK
Much of the 854 lb (388 kg) of rock collected on the Moon is volcanic. It dates from around 3.5 billion years ago.

Neil Armstrong (left) and Buzz Aldrin (right), the first men on the Moon

John Young was the commander of Apollo 16

THE TIMES

Senator Kennedy to be charged

Man lands on moon in perfect touchdown

Suez moves nearer to full-scale war

It looks like a collection of about every kind of rock, Armstrong reports

Who lives in an ivory tower?

HEADLINES AROUND THE WORLD
The world held its breath in July 1969 as Apollo 11 neared the Moon's surface. The successful landing was reported in newspapers and on the radio and television all over the world. Many people watched the landing on public screens, others at home. In Tokyo, Japan, stores sold out of color televisions in a prelaunch rush.

APOLLO 16 MOON LANDING
The Apollo craft landed at six different sites. The first three landings were close to the Moon's equator, but later missions carried more fuel and traveled farther. Apollo 16 touched down in the hilly Descartes region, where John Young and Charles Duke explored for three days. Each Apollo landing module had a code name. The Apollo 11 module, the first to reach the Moon, was called Eagle. Apollo 16's lander was Orion.

SUSPENDED
In addition to learning about spacecraft systems and the theory of working in space, astronauts practice tasks in space conditions. They learn what it is like to be in weightless conditions by scuba training or by using equipment like this harness, which helps them get used to floating free.

How to be an astronaut

MEN AND WOMEN ARE CHOSEN from around the world to train for traveling in space. They are launched aboard the US space shuttle, the Russian Soyuz rocket, or China's Long March rocket. The preparations for all space crews are similar and involve classroom and practical training, including work in mock-ups of the orbiter and parts of the International Space Station (ISS). They also involve training in simulators such as the harness, the 5DF machine, the moon-walker, and the multi-axis wheel, examples of which are found at the Euro Space Center, Transinne, Belgium, and are shown on these two pages. Astronauts can be selected for training every two years or so. A year's basic training is usually followed by training related to an astronaut's role in space, such as a pilot or a mission specialist who performs extra-vehicular activity (EVA). Only then do the successful astronauts get assigned to a flight.

Harness helps the astronaut get used to floating free

Three Apollo astronauts in training before their flights to the Moon

JUNGLE EMERGENCY
Astronauts are trained for any kind of situation or emergency. These astronauts are gathering leaves and branches to make a shelter after a pretend emergency landing in the middle of the Panama jungle. Even after landing on Earth, an astronaut's journey may not be over.

MOON-WALKER
Walking in a bulky spacesuit is difficult, particularly on the Moon, where gravity is one-sixth of Earth's. The Apollo astronauts found bunny hops the best way to get around the lunar surface. Future trips to the Moon or to Mars can be prepared for by walking in a moon-walker, a suspended chair.

LIFE RAFT
Astronaut candidates receive training in parachute jumping and land and sea survival. Here, US astronaut Leroy Chiao floats in his life raft in training for an emergency departure from the space shuttle.

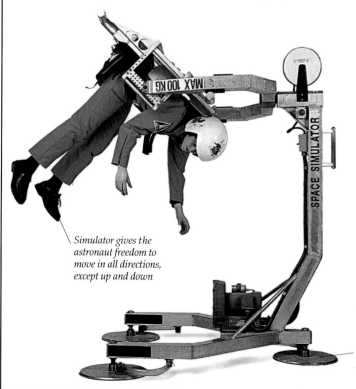

FIVE DEGREES OF FREEDOM
Preparing for the weightlessness of space is not easy. The feeling can be simulated in a chair called the Five Degrees of Freedom (5DF) machine, which allows the astronaut to move in all directions, other than up and down, without restraint. Alternatively, astronauts can get a 20- to 30-second taste of weightlessness aboard a modified KC-135 jet aircraft as it dives from 35,000 ft (10,700 m) to 24,000 ft (7,315 m). But the experience is brief, even though it can be repeated up to 40 times a day.

Simulator gives the astronaut freedom to move in all directions, except up and down

Three feet float over the floor, simulating movement achieved in frictionless space

UNDERWATER WEIGHTLESSNESS
Spacesuited astronauts can train for EVA in large water tanks, where the sensation of gravity is reduced. Space shuttle astronauts train with full-scale models of the orbiter payload bay and various payloads. Here, engineers work on a space station mock-up in preparation for astronaut training.

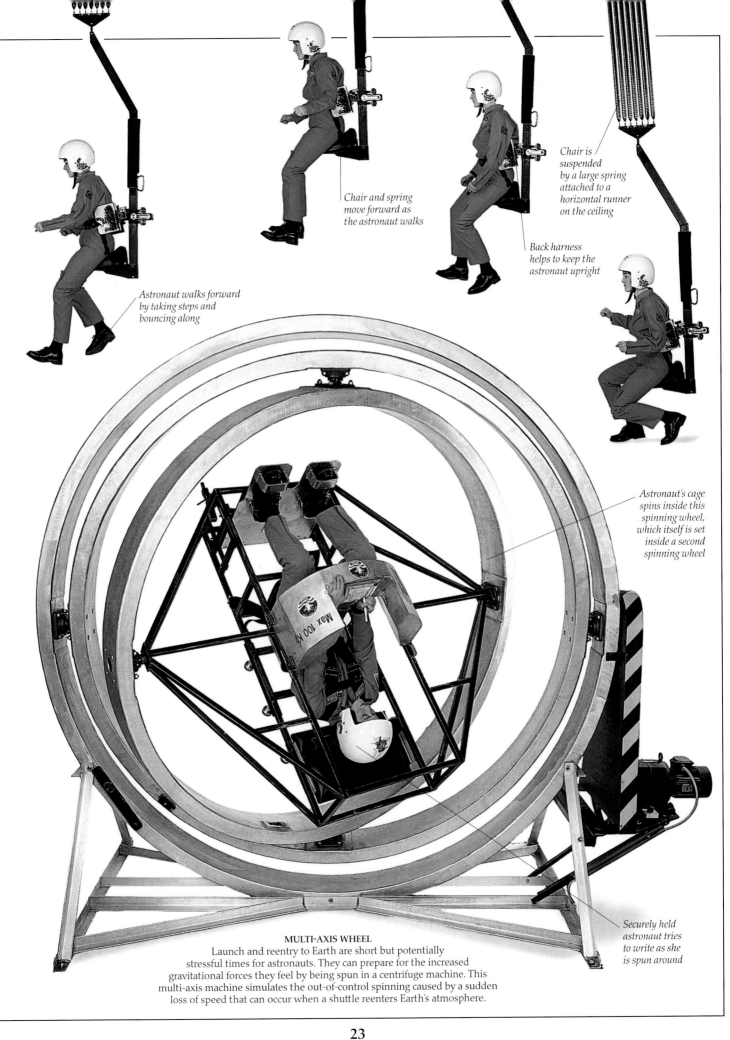

Chair is suspended by a large spring attached to a horizontal runner on the ceiling

Chair and spring move forward as the astronaut walks

Back harness helps to keep the astronaut upright

Astronaut walks forward by taking steps and bouncing along

Astronaut's cage spins inside this spinning wheel, which itself is set inside a second spinning wheel

Securely held astronaut tries to write as she is spun around

MULTI-AXIS WHEEL
Launch and reentry to Earth are short but potentially
stressful times for astronauts. They can prepare for the increased
gravitational forces they feel by being spun in a centrifuge machine. This
multi-axis machine simulates the out-of-control spinning caused by a sudden
loss of speed that can occur when a shuttle reenters Earth's atmosphere.

Astronaut fashion

A SPACESUIT IS LIKE a protective, portable tent that an astronaut wears to shield him in space. The first suits were designed for astronauts who were simply flying through space without leaving their craft. The suit they were launched in stayed on during eating, sleeping, going to the bathroom, and the return journey. Next came the suit for space itself. This provided the astronaut with a life-support system and protection against temperature extremes and space dust. Before going outside, the suit is pressurized to guard against the near vacuum of space. Today's astronauts wear suits for launch, work outside, and return. Inside, they wear casual, normal clothes.

Male underwear, designed for thermal control, 1960s

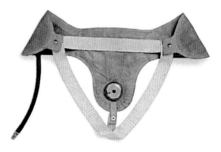

Device for collecting urine for male astronauts, early 1960s

Urine transferred from here

SPACE UNDERWEAR
Coping with human waste presents a tricky design problem. Any collecting device needs to keep the astronaut comfortable but dry at the same time. Collecting devices were essential for astronauts on early craft without toilets and, today, for long periods spent outside the craft.

MOBILE MAN
The first spacesuits were based on high-altitude pressure suits worn in jet aircraft. Astronauts wearing them had to be able to bend their arms and legs. The Apollo suits for the Moon had bellowlike molded rubber joints. The design has been simplified in this toy from 1966.

Portable life-support system

Suit of Yuri Gagarin, the first man in space, in 1961

Aleksei Leonov's suit, the first to be used outside spacecraft, in 1965

Mir space station suit, used in the late 1980s

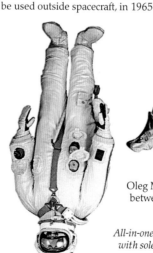

Oleg Makarov's suit, used between 1973 and 1980

All-in-one overshoe with sole and heel

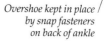

Overshoe kept in place by snap fasteners on back of ankle

CHANGING FASHION
A spacesuit's main job is to protect an astronaut. But it must also allow him to move around easily. These two basic requirements have not changed since the first astronaut flew. Yet, as the suits here show, spacesuit design has changed. New materials and techniques and practical experience combine to produce a comfortable and efficient suit for today's working astronaut. A suit is no longer tailor-made for one person but off-the-rack, and can be reused by another astronaut.

Oxygen passed to helmet through channels in internal surface

Visor's gold coating reflected heat and light

LOUSMA

Outer helmet

Pressure helmet

Communications cap

Pen-light pocket

DESIGNED FOR THE MOON
The Apollo suits were designed for use on the Moon. Closest to the skin, the astronaut wore a one-piece lightweight garment with sensors for monitoring changes in his body. Next was a garment with a network of over 300 ft (91 m) of tubing with constantly circulating cool water to maintain the astronaut's correct body heat. On top came the suit made of high-strength synthetic fibers, metals, and plastics. A portable life-support system was added on the back and controlled from the chest of the suit when the astronauts went outside their craft.

Two-piece underwear of long-sleeved vest and full-length pants

One-piece suit and underwear worn under spacesuit for launch and return home

Flag of Great Britain

X. ШАРМАН
H. SHARMAN

Unisex one-piece has under-leg zipper for quick waste removal

Outer glove placed over an inner pressure glove

IN-FLIGHT SPACE CLOTHES
Astronauts now have a selection of clothes they can wear inside a spacecraft. In the warm, safe atmosphere of a shuttle orbiter or a space station, astronauts wear unisex T-shirts and shorts or sweat pants. Socks keep feet warm, but there is no need for shoes. Helen Sharman's in-flight clothes included this one-piece sleeveless suit and jacket. In fact, it was far too warm on Mir to wear them together when she stayed on the station in 1991.

GEMINI SUIT
A member of the team that designed and made the suits for the US astronauts in the 1960s tests out a Gemini suit. It was worn by the first Americans to walk in space outside their craft.

Outer layers offered protection against temperature extremes and space dust

Foot straps held pants in place

Pocket contents secured by zipper

Living in space

Aʟʟ ᴛʜᴇ ᴛʜɪɴɢs ᴛʜᴀᴛ ᴡᴇ ᴅᴏ on Earth to stay alive are also done by astronauts in space. Astronauts still need to eat, breathe, sleep, keep clean and healthy, and use the bathroom. Everything needed for these activities is transported into, or made in, space. The main difference between life on Earth and in space is weightlessness. Seemingly simple, everyday tasks, such as breathing inside the craft, need to be carefully thought out. As the astronauts use up oxygen and breathe out carbon dioxide, they are in danger of suffocating. Fresh oxygen is circulated around the craft. Water vapor from the astronauts' breath is collected and recycled for use in experiments and for drinking. Air rather than water is used to suck, and not flush, body wastes away.

CUTTING EDGE
Astronauts spending weeks or months in space cut each other's hair. The hair cuttings do not settle, so they must be sucked up before they spread through the spacecraft.

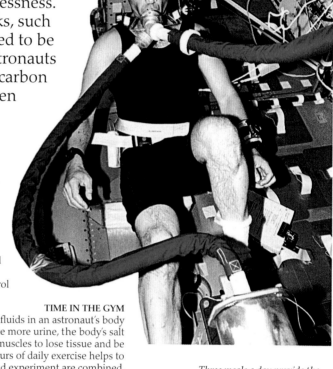

UNDER PRESSURE
Body fluids are no longer pulled down by gravity and move up toward an astronaut's head. For the first few days, his face looks fatter and his nasal passages are blocked. Belts worn at the top of each leg help control the flow until the body adjusts itself.

TIME IN THE GYM
The upward movement of fluids in an astronaut's body causes the kidneys to excrete more urine, the body's salt concentration to be upset, and muscles to lose tissue and be less able to work. About two hours of daily exercise helps to counteract this. Here, exercise and experiment are combined. As Canadian Robert Thirsk pedals, his condition is monitored.

Three meals a day provide the astronaut with the required intake of 2,800 calories

Sweet and sour beef

Pineapple

Peach

Drinks

Rice

Pear

WHAT'S ON THE MENU?
Meals are prepared long before launch. Packaged foods can be ready to eat, may need warming, or may need water added. Many foods, such as cornflakes, meatballs, and lemon pudding, are similar to those on a supermarket shelf. Fresh foods are eaten at the start of a trip or when delivered by visiting astronauts.

Cereals

Food packages held on a tray, which is strapped to the astronaut's leg

Chicken

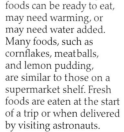

Fruit and nuts

Peas

Almonds

Holes in the cutlery handles mean they can be tied down

PERSONAL HYGIENE
Astronauts who flew to Mir were given a material pouch containing personal hygiene items. This one was issued to British astronaut Helen Sharman for her stay on board Mir in 1991. Individual pockets contain hair-, teeth-, and hand-care items. Teeth are cleaned with a brush and edible, nonfrothy toothpaste, or with special, moist finger wipe.

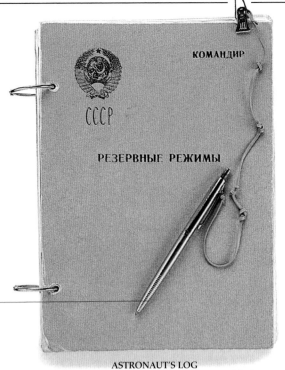

In pens designed for use in space, ink is pushed toward the nib. On Earth, gravity pulls ink down

ASTRONAUT'S LOG
An astronaut's log book contains details of flight procedures. Helen Sharman followed the launch, Mir-docking, and Earth-landing in hers. She flew to Mir on the Russian craft Soyuz TM-12. As part of her training, she had learned to speak Russian.

HIGH-FLYING BUTTERFLY
Everything an astronaut might need in space is provided by the space agency he or she is flying with. But astronauts do have the chance to take a personal item or two with them. These must be small and light. Helen Sharman carried this brooch given to her by her father.

Body-washing wipe

SPACE SHOWER
The first private toilet and shower were on the US space station Skylab, which was in space from 1973 to 1974. The toilet was unreliable and the shower leaked, so the astronauts had to spend precious time cleaning up. Astronauts on the International Space Station take sponge baths using two cloths, one for washing and one for rinsing. They wash their hair with rinseless shampoo.

KEEPING CLEAN
Wet wipes are used to clean astronauts' bodies and the inside of the spacecraft. Some, like these Russian ones, are specially made for use in space. Others are commercial baby wipes.

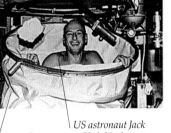

US astronaut Jack Lousma uses Skylab's shower

Inside the sealed unit, water is air-blasted at the astronaut and immediately sucked up

Handle for the astronaut to hold himself down

Astronaut sits here. The toilet seat is lifted up for cleaning

Toilet is cut away to show how the solid waste is collected

WASTE MANAGEMENT
On entering the toilet, an astronaut puts on a rubber glove and chooses a funnel. Once this is attached to the waste hose, he sits down and holds the funnel close to his body. The toilet fan is turned on and, as the astronaut urinates, the liquid is drawn through the hose by air. Before discarding solid waste, the toilet bowl is pressurized to produce a tight seal between the astronaut and the seat. Finally, the astronaut cleans himself and the toilet with wipes.

Male or female funnel is held close to the astronaut to collect liquid waste

Hose takes away liquid waste

Feet are secured on the footrests

Model of a space toilet at the Euro Space Center, Transinne, Belgium

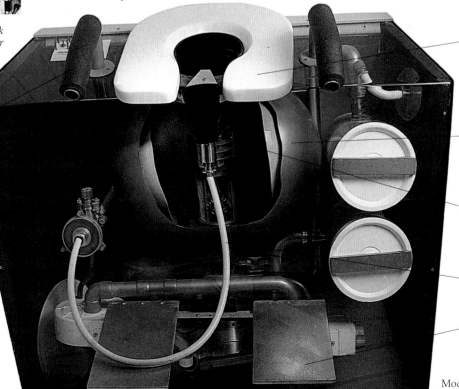

Astronauts at work

A WORKING DAY FOR AN ASTRONAUT could be spent inside or outside his craft. Inside, routine monitoring and maintenance on the craft is carried out alongside scientific testing and experimentation. This can include investigation of the effects of space travel on the human body, testing of new products in space, and research into food production, which will benefit future space generations. Commercial organizations send experiments into space to be performed in weightlessness. Work outside is called extra-vehicular activity (EVA). An astronaut will be secured to his craft by a tether, or attached to a moveable mechanical arm. He might deploy satellites, set up experiments, or help build the International Space Station (ISS).

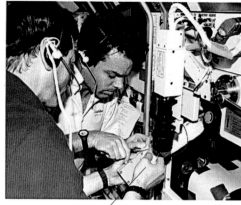

Repair of the Bubble Drop Particle Unit

RUNNING REPAIRS
In-flight repairs had to be made to an experiment unit on board the shuttle Columbia. Back on Earth, Spanish astronaut Pedro Duque carried out the very same repair procedure. His work was recorded, and the video pictures were transmitted to the in-flight crew, Frenchman Jean-Jacques Favier and American Kevin Kregel, who then did the real repair.

ORDERS FROM BELOW
Astronauts are assigned tasks on a mission long before they leave Earth. They work closely with the scientists and engineers who have designed and produced experiments in the months prior to launch. While the astronauts are in space, the scientists wait on Earth for the successful completion of the mission. Once they stayed in touch through the teleprinter, but laptops are more convenient today.

Goggles and headgear examine how the astronaut orientates

US astronaut Richard Linnehan in Spacelab aboard Columbia

Challenger was filled with hundreds of yards worth of teleprinter paper in 1985

LOOK AFTER YOURSELF
For some work, the astronaut is both the scientist and the subject of his investigation. His job is to see how the human body—his own body—copes with the space environment. On Earth, gravity pulls things toward its surface and so provides a visual reference for up and down. In space, there is no up and down and this can be very disorientating.

Astronaut prepares samples in the glove box

WORKING IN A GLOVE BOX
Experiments from around the world have been conducted in Mir and in Spacelab (right), the European laboratory carried on the shuttle. Some only needed to be activated when in space, others needed more direct participation by an astronaut. US astronaut Leroy Chiao (top) places samples in one of the centrifuges on board. American Donald Thomas's hands are in the glove box, a sealed experiment unit.

Securing pins

Sheet cutters

Bolt tightener

Wire cutters

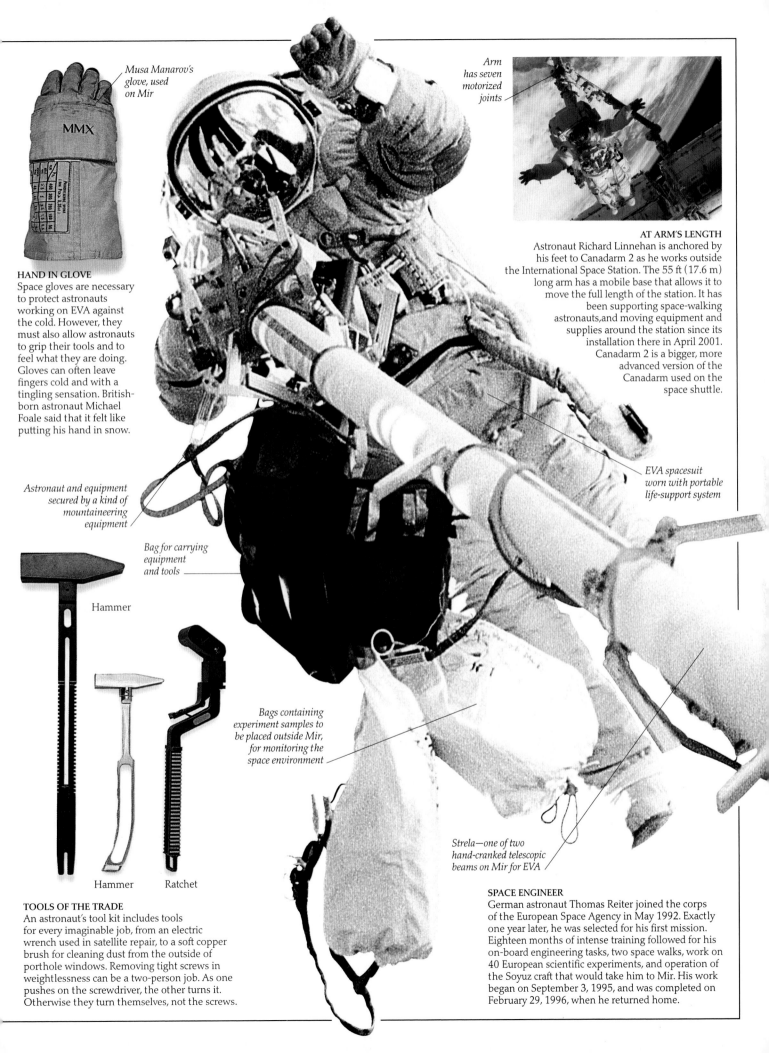

HAND IN GLOVE
Space gloves are necessary to protect astronauts working on EVA against the cold. However, they must also allow astronauts to grip their tools and to feel what they are doing. Gloves can often leave fingers cold and with a tingling sensation. British-born astronaut Michael Foale said that it felt like putting his hand in snow.

Musa Manarov's glove, used on Mir

MMX

Arm has seven motorized joints

AT ARM'S LENGTH
Astronaut Richard Linnehan is anchored by his feet to Canadarm 2 as he works outside the International Space Station. The 55 ft (17.6 m) long arm has a mobile base that allows it to move the full length of the station. It has been supporting space-walking astronauts,and moving equipment and supplies around the station since its installation there in April 2001. Canadarm 2 is a bigger, more advanced version of the Canadarm used on the space shuttle.

EVA spacesuit worn with portable life-support system

Astronaut and equipment secured by a kind of mountaineering equipment

Bag for carrying equipment and tools

Hammer

Hammer   **Ratchet**

TOOLS OF THE TRADE
An astronaut's tool kit includes tools for every imaginable job, from an electric wrench used in satellite repair, to a soft copper brush for cleaning dust from the outside of porthole windows. Removing tight screws in weightlessness can be a two-person job. As one pushes on the screwdriver, the other turns it. Otherwise they turn themselves, not the screws.

Bags containing experiment samples to be placed outside Mir, for monitoring the space environment

Strela—one of two hand-cranked telescopic beams on Mir for EVA

SPACE ENGINEER
German astronaut Thomas Reiter joined the corps of the European Space Agency in May 1992. Exactly one year later, he was selected for his first mission. Eighteen months of intense training followed for his on-board engineering tasks, two space walks, work on 40 European scientific experiments, and operation of the Soyuz craft that would take him to Mir. His work began on September 3, 1995, and was completed on February 29, 1996, when he returned home.

Rest and play

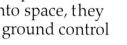

Yo-yo thrown out sideways comes back without gravity pulling it down

Astronauts have leisure time in space just as they would if they were down on Earth. When the day's work is finished, they might like to indulge in a favorite pastime of reading, photography, or music, or join together for a game of cards. Whatever their preference, they are bound to spend some time simply gazing out of the spacecraft window. Watching the world far below is a pastime no astronaut tires of. When the first astronauts went into space, they had every moment of their time accounted for and ground control was always listening in. Time to unwind and enjoy the experience and unique sensations space offers is now in every astronaut's timetable.

SEEING SHARKS
US astronaut Bill Lenoir watches his floating rubber shark.

WRITING HOME
Laptop computers can help astronauts stay in touch with family and friends on a day-to-day basis. Others prefer to write letters home. Astronauts on Mir operated their own post office. Letters were stamped and dated when written and handed over when the astronaut got back to Earth. This French stamp for Earth-use celebrated communications.

Jacks float in midair as there is no gravity to keep them on a surface

A chain of seven magnetic marbles is achieved on Earth before gravity pulls them apart

In space, because the marbles are weightless, you can keep on adding to the chain

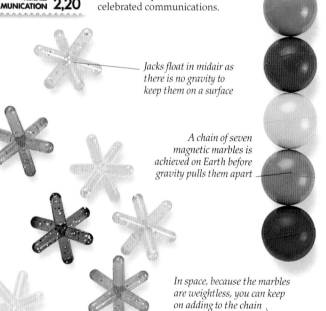

STAY STILL!
On Earth, jacks are picked up in increasing numbers from the floor as the ball is thrown up and caught. In space, the jacks are released in midair but always drift apart. The ball is thrown at a spacecraft wall and caught on its return journey.

Drink flows out independently unless the mouthpiece is sealed between sips

SNACKTIME
Hungry astronauts have a choice of food snacks and drinks to keep them going between meals. Dried fruit, nuts, crumb-free snack bars, and hot or cold drinks supplement their diet. Drinks are usually taken from sealed packs or tubes. Once this soda can is opened in space, the drink can flow out freely, so it requires a special mouthpiece.

Guitar collapses for easy storage

German astronaut Thomas Reiter during his 179-day stay on Mir

COSMIC CHORDS
Music CDs are light and small, two important qualities for any nonessential item carried into space. Singing along can be fun, but as one astronaut relaxes, another is still working hard nearby, so the volume cannot be too high. Sometimes a change of music is supplied by visiting astronauts. In November 1995, an Atlantis crew briefly docked with Mir, leaving behind a gift of a collapsible guitar.

SPACE TOYS

Ten familiar toys were packed aboard the space shuttle Discovery when it blasted into space in April 1985. These 10, plus one more the astronauts made in space, a paper airplane, became the stars of an educational video. The mid-deck became a classroom as the astronauts demonstrated the toys, including a yo-yo, jacks, and magnetic marbles.

Hair only moves upward if pushed

HAIR-RAISING

Washing clothes and hair are not top priorities in space. Clothes are bagged and brought home dirty. Hair washing can be avoided if the trip is short. If it needs to be washed, it cannot be done in the usual way, with lots of water and shampoo. Dirt can be wiped away by a cloth impregnated with a shampoo-like substance.

American Susan Helms tests space shampoo

Wubbo Ockels from the Netherlands on board the shuttle Challenger in 1985

Inflatable ring provided support for the sleeping astronaut

Woolen slippers gave Ockels extra warmth and comfort

SPACE PHOTOGRAPHER

Taking photographs in space is one way to keep a unique memory alive. Digital cameras and camcorders are on board the spacecraft. In addition to making an official record of the trip, astronauts take fun shots. Here, American Karl Henize photographs through the window of the Challenger shuttle orbiter to catch the scene in the payload bay outside.

Sleeping bag designed by Ockels

GOOD NIGHT, SLEEP TIGHT

Astronauts once slept in their seats or in temporarily hung hammocks. Today, they have a more comfortable choice. Sleeping bags are attached to the sides of the spacecraft, or a sound-suppression blanket and sheets with weightlessness restraints are used in a private bunk bed. This special sleeping bag was used in the 1980s aboard the space shuttle and Mir. Its inflatable ring simulated the pressure that the weight of bedclothes provides on Earth.

Danger and disaster

GREAT CARE IS TAKEN IN THE PLANNING and preparation of a space mission. Once a rocket and its cargo leave the ground, there is little anyone can do if things go terribly wrong. The smallest error can mean the end of a billion-dollar project. Years of work and the hopes and expectations of hundreds of people can be lost in a second. Mistakes can happen and problems do arise. They range from an astronaut's cold that delayed a flight, through whole projects that failed, to the loss of life. But big disasters are rare, and we are incredibly successful at sending craft and astronauts into space.

NEIGHBORS
The American shuttle launch center is in Florida, next to a wildlife refuge. The osprey is one of over 300 species of bird in the area. Space technicians check regularly that the birds do not nest in the wrong place.

PARACHUTE PROBLEM
Vladimir Komarov was the first human to be killed in space flight. After a day in space, he descended to Earth on April 24, 1967. The lines of his Soyuz 1 parachute became tangled, and the parachute deflated. The craft plunged to the ground and burst into flames.

The Apollo 13 crew is honored. The mission was regarded as a successful failure because of the rescue experience gained

President Nixon welcomes home the crew of Apollo 13

MISSION ABORT
On April 13, 1970, two days after launch, Apollo 13's journey to the Moon was interrupted when an oxygen tank ruptured and caused an explosion that damaged power and life-support systems on board. The major incident was calmly reported to Earth with the words "Houston, we've had a problem here." The planned lunar landing was abandoned and every effort was channeled into getting the three-man crew home safely.

John Swigert   Fred Haise   James Lovell   Richard Nixon

HOME AT LAST
The explosion aboard Apollo 13 was in the service module and put its engine out of action. The astronauts used the engine of the lunar module, originally intended for maneuver on and off the Moon, to take them around the Moon and return them to Earth. Everyone was relieved as the astronauts were lifted aboard the recovery ship.

FLASH FIRE
US astronauts Virgil Grissom, Edward White, and Roger Chaffee perished in a fire in the command module of Apollo 1 on January 27, 1967. They were on the ground practicing launch countdown and could not open the module hatch to escape. As a result, spacecraft were redesigned.

Urns holding the remains of the astronauts were placed in the Kremlin wall

Effects of the intense heat can be seen on the outside of the command module

RETURN FROM SPACE
After a 23-day stay on the Salyut 1 space station, Soviet astronauts Georgi Dobrovolsky, Vladislav Volkov, and Viktor Patsayev started their journey home. As they approached Earth on June 30, 1971, air escaped from their capsule. The three were not wearing spacesuits. They suffocated and were found dead when their capsule landed.

Astronauts test launch pad emergency exit in a dress rehearsal for their launch

One of seven baskets. Each basket can hold three crew members and has its own wire system to carry them safely to the ground

ESCAPE ROUTE

Emergency procedures have been developed to allow astronauts to get away from their craft quickly. For shuttle astronauts, the escape route before the final 30 seconds of countdown is via a steel-wire basket. It takes 35 seconds to slide to the ground, practiced here. On arrival, the astronauts move to an emergency bunker until they get the all-clear.

LOST IN SPACE

In February 1996, astronauts were putting a satellite into space when the 12.8 mile (20.6 km) tether that connected it to the space shuttle Columbia snapped. The $442 million satellite had to be given up as lost. Astronauts had unsuccessfully tried to deploy the Italian satellite four years earlier. Once deployed, the satellite would have been swept through Earth's magnetic field to generate electricity.

With only about 30 ft (10 m) to go, the tether broke and the satellite was lost

SPACE SHUTTLE TRAGEDIES

Launch-pad preparation and liftoff are among the most dangerous parts of a mission. Seventy-three seconds after liftoff on January 28, 1986, the space shuttle Challenger exploded. All seven of the crew were killed. This was the first flight to take off and not reach space. Disaster struck the shuttle fleet a second time in 2003, but not at liftoff. This time, the Columbia shuttle disintegrated as it returned to Earth, again with the loss of the entire crew.

Mars-96 was assembled at the Lavochkin Scientific-Industrial Association, Khimki, near Moscow

MARS-96

The Russian space probe Mars-96 was launched successfully from the Baikonur Cosmodrome on November 16, 1996, but, about half an hour after takeoff, contact with the probe was lost. The fourth set of boosters had failed to lift Mars-96 out of Earth's orbit and on toward its target, Mars.

PECKING PROBLEM

A yellow-shafted flicker woodpecker delayed the launch of the space shuttle in June 1995. Discovery was ready for liftoff on the launch pad but had to be returned to its hangar at a cost of $100,000.

The bird had pecked more than 75 holes in the fuel tank's insulating foam. Plastic owls to scare off birds are among the measures now taken to avoid a repetition on the problem.

Experiment box recovered from swamps in French Guiana, near the launch site of Ariane 5

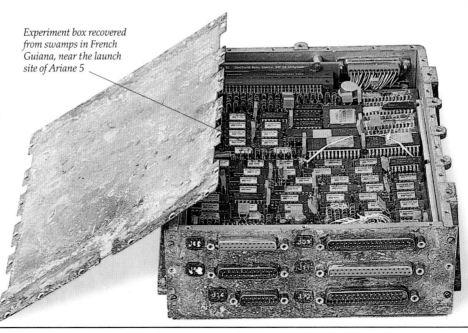

LOST PROPERTY

The failure of Mars-96 was a serious setback for the exploration of Mars and the Russian space program. The probe had been scheduled to land four probes on Mars in September 1997. The loss of experiments on this probe came only five months after the destruction of experiments carried on the European Space Agency rocket Ariane 5, which blew up soon after launch as a result of a computer software problem.

Space stations

ABOUT 220 MILES (354 KM) ABOVE THE EARTH, astronauts are constructing the International Space Station (ISS). When completed, it will be the largest and most complex space station ever built. It is is the latest of 10 space stations. The first was the Russian Salyut 1, put in orbit in 1971. Six more Salyuts followed. The United States station Skylab was used in the mid-1970s. Prior to the ISS, the most successful station was Mir, Russia's eighth. Astronauts stayed on Mir for months at a time. They conducted experiments, made observations, and collected valuable data on how humans cope with long spells in space. The record for the longest unbroken stay by one person in space was made on Mir.

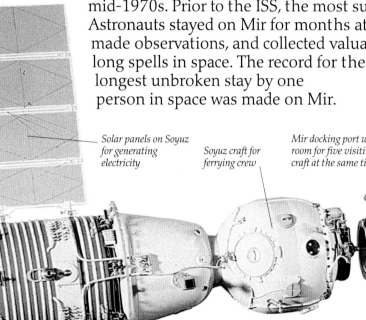

First Mir module into space. The crew lived here

Solar panels on Soyuz for generating electricity

Soyuz craft for ferrying crew

Mir docking port with room for five visiting craft at the same time

MIR—A SUCCESSFUL STATION

Mir was constructed in space between 1986 and 1996. New parts were added to the original living module piece by piece. This model shows how it looked in 1988. A photo at the bottom right shows Mir in 1995, before the final module was added. Astronauts occupied Mir almost continuously from February 1987 to June 2000. There were usually two or three crew on board, but Mir could take up to six astronauts. They came from more than a dozen countries, arriving by Soyuz craft or shuttle orbiter. Mir was brought out of orbit and broke up in Earth's atmosphere in March 2001.

Artsebarski stayed on Mir for 145 days, Krikalev (right) for 310 days

FIRST STEPS TO SPACE

Three astronauts walk across the Baikonur Cosmodrome launch site toward their Soyuz TM-12 rocket to take them to Mir in May 1991. Helen Sharman (left)—the first Briton to go into space and the first woman on Mir—stayed on board for eight days. The commander, Anatoli Artsebarski, was flying for the first time. But flight engineer Sergei Krikalev (right) was familiar with Mir, as he had stayed there two years earlier.

Spacesuits are fireproof, waterproof, airtight, and ventilated. The helmet goes on last

THE HIGH LIFE
The seventh and final Salyut space station was launched in April 1982. Salyut 7 was in orbit, about 200 miles (320 km) above Earth, until February 1991. The first crew members were Anatoly Berezovoi (top) and Valentin Lebedev (bottom); they spent 211 days in space, setting a record. Salyut 7 was also home to the first male-female space crew.

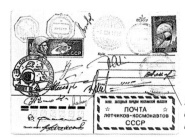

POSTCARD FROM SPACE
Cards like this one have been through a post office that was truly out of this world—the one on board Mir. The office's unique postmark was stamped by hand. The crew aboard Mir in late 1987 stamped and signed about 1,000 envelopes for stamp collectors around the world.

Sergei Avdeev stayed on Mir from September 1995 to February 1996

Signatures of all the Mir astronauts

INSIDE MIR
The inside of Mir was similar in size and shape to the interior of a train car. There was no floor or ceiling, so in every direction you looked there was equipment for the operation of the space station, for experiments, or for the astronauts' day-to-day needs.

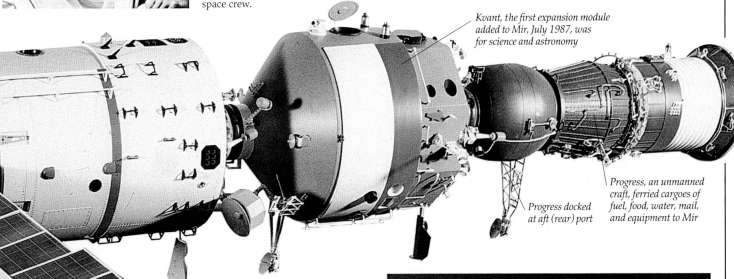

Kvant, the first expansion module added to Mir, July 1987, was for science and astronomy

Progress docked at aft (rear) port

Progress, an unmanned craft, ferried cargoes of fuel, food, water, mail, and equipment to Mir

SPACE UNION
In June 1995, the US space shuttle orbiter made its first docking with Russia's Mir. At the time, they formed the largest craft ever to have orbited Earth. The crew members aboard the US craft Atlantis had their own celebration—they were the 100th American human space launch.

Photograph of Atlantis moving away from Mir taken by Solovyev and Budarin, who temporarily left Mir in their Soyuz spacecraft

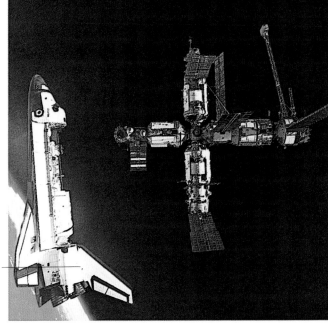

HITCHING A RIDE
Anatoly Solovyev and Nikolai Budarin were taken to Mir aboard Atlantis. Once the orbiter had docked with Mir, the hatches on each side were opened. Solovyev and Budarin and the five US astronauts passed through to Mir for a welcoming ceremony. Five days later, Atlantis, carrying the Americans, left Mir, leaving the other two astronauts behind.

FOND FAREWELL
Atlantis and Mir were docked together for about 100 hours as they orbited Earth in June 1995. On board were the seven astronauts who had arrived on Atlantis, and three other astronauts who were already on board Mir. These three prepared for reentry into gravity after more than three months in space. They returned to Earth aboard Atlantis, along with medical samples they had taken while in space.

Science without gravity

ASTRONAUTS MONITOR, control, and perform experiments inside and outside their craft as they orbit Earth. The experiments are provided by space agencies, industry, universities, and by schools. They may be concerned with finding out how living things, such as astronauts, insects, and plants, cope in space. They also cover areas such as chemical processes and the behavior of materials. The knowledge acquired is used for planning the space future, or is applied to life on Earth. Experiments may be only a part of a crew's workload, or the whole reason for a space mission.

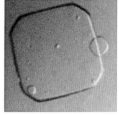

CRYSTAL
This crystal of human-body plasma protein was grown in space. Crystals grown in space are larger and better ordered than those grown on Earth. Studying them provides knowledge that can be used to help treat diseases.

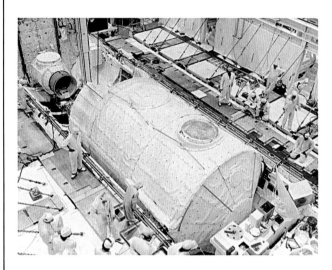

Bondar checks on oat seedlings in an experiment box aboard Discovery

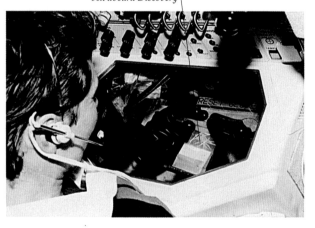

SPACELAB
A laboratory designed for space, Spacelab flies in the payload bay of the space shuttle. Astronauts work in its pressurized cabin, and U-shaped pallets on the outside of the the cabin hold instruments for direct exposure to space. Spacelab first flew in 1983. An average flight lasts 10 days. Here, the laboratory is being installed in the shuttle's payload bay before a flight.

GROWING FOOD
A self-contained plant-growth unit was used in March 1982 to test how weightlessness affects plants. These two sets of seedlings were grown from seeds in the unit aboard the space shuttle Columbia. They grew to look much the same as seedlings growing on Earth, although a few small roots grew upward.

Oat seedlings

EXPERIMENT IN A BOX
Canadian Roberta Bondar was one of seven astronauts performing experiments on an eight-day shuttle flight in January 1992. Their research included studying the effects of weightlessness on lentil and oat seedlings and on shrimp and fruitfly eggs.

Mung bean seedlings

BABY BOOM
The first Earth creature to be born in space emerged from its shell on March 22, 1990. The quail chick was the result of an experiment aboard Mir. Forty-eight Japanese quails' eggs had been flown to the space station and placed inside a special incubator with ventilation, feeding, heating, waste, and storage systems attached. Then astronauts on Mir and scientists on Earth waited. On the 17th day, the first eggs began to crack open and six chicks broke free, one after the other. Although the birth made little impact beyond the world of space biologists, it marked a key moment in research into reproduction in space, which will be used to plan the space future.

Quail's egg with crack
as it begins to hatch

Chick's feathers
appear as egg breaks

WORKING TOGETHER—THE EXPERIMENT
Astronauts often perform experiments in space for Earth-based scientists. Here, British scientist John Parkinson (right) instructs US astronaut Karl Henize, who will be in charge of his telescope in space. They are checking the controls for pointing the telescope at the correct part of the Sun.

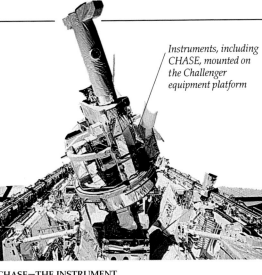

Instruments, including CHASE, mounted on the Challenger equipment platform

CHASE—THE INSTRUMENT
The second Spacelab mission, which flew aboard Challenger in summer 1985, included the telescope of John Parkinson (see right) in the orbiter payload bay. The telescope, called the Coronal Helium Abundance Spacelab Experiment (CHASE), measured how much helium there is in the Sun's outer layers.

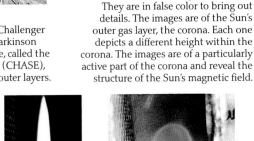

SOLAR IMAGES—THE RESULTS
CHASE made these images of the Sun. They are in false color to bring out details. The images are of the Sun's outer gas layer, the corona. Each one depicts a different height within the corona. The images are of a particularly active part of the corona and reveal the structure of the Sun's magnetic field.

ALL IN A DAY'S WORK
The French astronaut Jean-Jacques Favier works on an experiment while wearing the Torso Rotation Experiment, which is one of a series of experiments used to study the effects of weightlessness on the human body. Favier and other crew members in the Life and Microgravity Spacelab aboard Columbia in 1996 were also tested for bone tissue loss, muscle performance, and energy expenditure.

Richard Linnehan, an American, tests his muscle response with the handgrip equipment

Astronauts use footgrips to keep themselves steady as they work

Torso Rotation Experiment

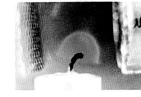

CANDLE FLAMES
It is known that factors such as gravity and airflow influence the spread of an Earth fire, but what might affect a space fire? Tests have shown that space flames form a sphere, rather than the pointed shape they have on Earth (left). They also lean strongly when subjected to an electric field (right), which leaves Earth flames unaffected.

Arabella in the web she built on board Skylab

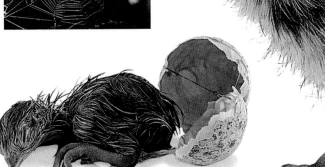

ARABELLA THE SPIDER
One space science experiment was designed by a high-school student from Massachusetts. It involved two spiders, Anita and Arabella. The student wanted to find out how well they could make webs in weightless conditions. Their first attempts at web spinning were not perfect, but once space-adapted, the spiders built strong and well-organized webs.

Chick squeezes out of broken egg

Eggshell falls away as chick hatches

Quail chick stands up

Testing equipment

Any equipment sent into space undergoes rigorous and lengthy tests long before it goes near the launch site. The process of building and testing for space starts years ahead of liftoff. Prototypes of each element of a space probe or satellite are individually built and thoroughly tested before moving on to produce the actual flight parts. About a year before launch, the parts are brought together for assembly. The whole craft is then put through another test cycle to ensure it is fully spaceworthy. It must be able to withstand the stress of launch and the environment once in space. The tests are therefore carried out in conditions as close as possible to those encountered in space.

Exterior of the Large Space Simulator (LSS), shown in detail below

Facilities for testing small- and medium-sized equipment

TESTING SPACECRAFT
At its Netherlands space center, the European Space Agency (ESA) monitors and analyzes the behavior of space probes and satellites to assess how spaceworthy the craft are. Something as simple as a speck of dust can cause a very costly short circuit later on, so the tests must be performed in controlled, clean conditions.

HUMAN TESTS
American John Bull tested a newly designed Apollo spacesuit for mobility in 1968. Bull later withdrew from training because of poor health and never made it into space. Men and women traveling into space also go through test procedures to make sure they are in good condition and will survive their trip.

ADAPTING TO SPACE
With more and longer space flights planned, astronauts are increasingly being tested for endurance and adaptability. They undergo tests before, during, and after flight. Tests are carried out on other humans for comparison. Volunteers are strapped down, wired up, and swung around to simulate the return from space to gravity.

Auxiliary chamber houses mirror

Mirror is made up of 121 pieces

LARGE SPACE SIMULATOR
The environmental conditions a craft will encounter in space are simulated by special test equipment. The European Space Agency (ESA) has been using the Large Space Simulator (LSS) since 1986 to test its space probes and satellites. It works by re-creating the vacuum, heat, and solar radiation conditions of space. The craft to be tested is sealed in the main chamber, which is depressurized to achieve a vacuum. The impact of the Sun is produced by lamps, with a large mirror directing the solar beam to the craft. This is a model of the LSS that allows you to see inside.

Light reflection from the Sun simulator is directed to the main chamber

Chambers have temperature-controlled stainless-steel shrouds

GAS GUN
Spacecraft need to be protected from miniscule particles of space dust, which can produce surface holes and craters when they collide with the craft. Scientists in Canterbury, England, use a gas gun to assess the damage such particles can cause. This research has provided valuable information for the design of spacecraft bumper shields.

Test using thin metal

Test using thick metal

BUMPER SHIELD
Scientists have tested different thicknesses of metal to find a way of minimizing the damage dust particles can do to space probes. A double-layer bumper shield can also help reduce damage. The first layer of metal breaks up the particle and spreads out the energy.

SOLAR PANELS
The effects of space dust are shown by comparing these solar panels. The panels on the right have not been used, while the panel on the left has been retrieved from space. The dents and pits caused by the impact of space particles can be seen clearly. Scientists can use this evidence to determine the size and speed of the space particles.

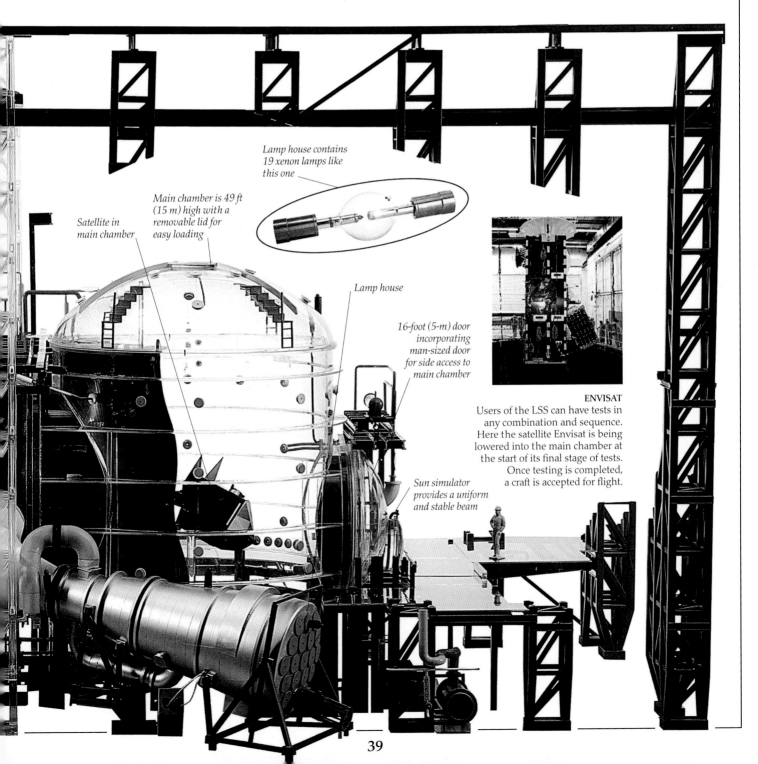

Lamp house contains 19 xenon lamps like this one

Satellite in main chamber

Main chamber is 49 ft (15 m) high with a removable lid for easy loading

Lamp house

16-foot (5-m) door incorporating man-sized door for side access to main chamber

Sun simulator provides a uniform and stable beam

ENVISAT
Users of the LSS can have tests in any combination and sequence. Here the satellite Envisat is being lowered into the main chamber at the start of its final stage of tests. Once testing is completed, a craft is accepted for flight.

Lonely explorers

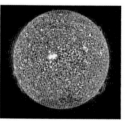

VOYAGER 1
Two Voyager craft toured Jupiter, Saturn, Uranus, and Neptune.

Sᴄɪᴇɴᴛɪsᴛs sᴏᴍᴇᴛɪᴍᴇs ᴇxᴘʟᴏʀᴇ sᴘᴀᴄᴇ using robotic spacecraft, which are launched from Earth by rocket or space shuttle to travel to a predetermined target. About the size of sedan cars, these craft, often called probes, contain scientific experiments to conduct investigations, a power supply, small thruster rockets for path adjustment, and a means for recording and sending data back to Earth. A probe may fly by its target, or orbit it, or land on it, or perform a combination of maneuvers. Some probes carry a second, smaller probe or lander craft for release into an atmosphere, or for touchdown on a planetary or lunar surface. Probes have investigated all eight solar system planets and many of their moons, as well as comets, asteroids, and the Sun.

SOAKING UP THE SUN
The Solar and Heliospheric Observatory (SOHO), the most comprehensive spacecraft to study the Sun, started its work in April 1996. Twelve different instruments on board the SOHO space probe are observing the Sun constantly.

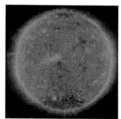  

SUNNY OUTLOOK
In visible light the Sun appears calm, but SOHO is recording plenty of vigorous activity. Every day, SOHO pictures the whole Sun at four ultraviolet wavelengths (shown here), which correspond to different temperatures in the Sun's atmosphere. SOHO was designed to operate until 1998, but new funding has extended its working life to at least December 2009.

Circles represent hydrogen atoms emitting radiation at a particular wavelength

Sketch of Pioneer, drawn to scale, with people to show the size of humans

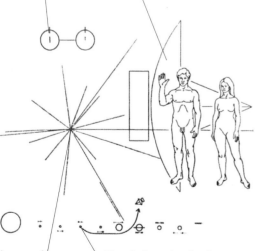

MESSAGE FROM EARTH
A few months before the launch of Pioneer 10 in 1972, it was realized that it and its sister probe, Pioneer 11, would follow paths that eventually would take them out of the solar system. It was agreed that the probes, traveling in opposite directions, should carry messages in case any extraterrestrials came across them in the future. The messages were etched on a 6 in (15 cm) x 9 in (23 cm) gold-covered aluminum plaque.

Boom with magnetometer to measure magnetic field in interplanetary space and near Jupiter

A means of locating the solar system in the Milky Way

Map of solar system showing Pioneer has come from the third planet (Earth) and passed close by Jupiter

BEYOND THE BELT
Pioneer 10 left Earth on March 3, 1972, for a journey to the planet Jupiter. It was the first probe to venture beyond the asteroid belt. It took six months to emerge at the far side, successfully avoiding a collision with a piece of space rock. The probe flew by Jupiter at a distance of 81,000 miles (130,300 km) before heading for the edge of the solar system. Space probes close to the Sun can use solar panels for power to operate and communicate with Earth. For travel beyond the planet Mars, like Pioneer 10, electric generators need to be on board.

View of Jupiter from Pioneer 10

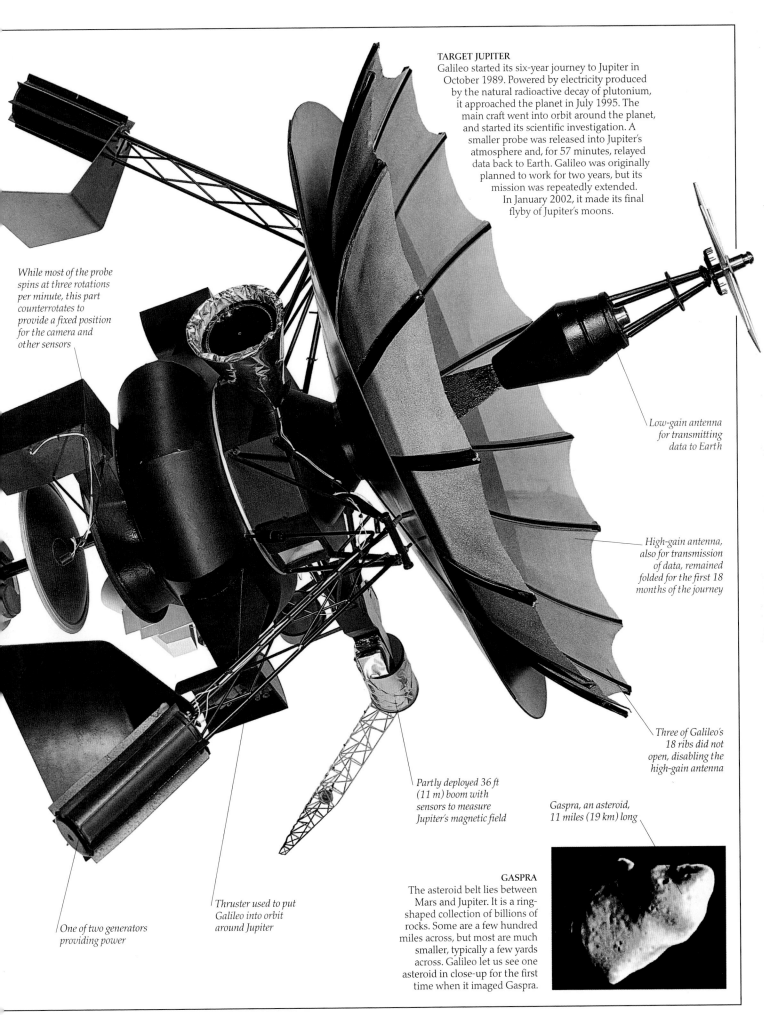

TARGET JUPITER
Galileo started its six-year journey to Jupiter in
October 1989. Powered by electricity produced
by the natural radioactive decay of plutonium,
it approached the planet in July 1995. The
main craft went into orbit around the planet,
and started its scientific investigation. A
smaller probe was released into Jupiter's
atmosphere and, for 57 minutes, relayed
data back to Earth. Galileo was originally
planned to work for two years, but its
mission was repeatedly extended.
In January 2002, it made its final
flyby of Jupiter's moons.

*While most of the probe
spins at three rotations
per minute, this part
counterrotates to
provide a fixed position
for the camera and
other sensors*

*Low-gain antenna
for transmitting
data to Earth*

*High-gain antenna,
also for transmission
of data, remained
folded for the first 18
months of the journey*

*Three of Galileo's
18 ribs did not
open, disabling the
high-gain antenna*

*Partly deployed 36 ft
(11 m) boom with
sensors to measure
Jupiter's magnetic field*

*Gaspra, an asteroid,
11 miles (19 km) long*

*One of two generators
providing power*

*Thruster used to put
Galileo into orbit
around Jupiter*

GASPRA
The asteroid belt lies between
Mars and Jupiter. It is a ring-
shaped collection of billions of
rocks. Some are a few hundred
miles across, but most are much
smaller, typically a few yards
across. Galileo let us see one
asteroid in close-up for the first
time when it imaged Gaspra.

41

In-depth investigators

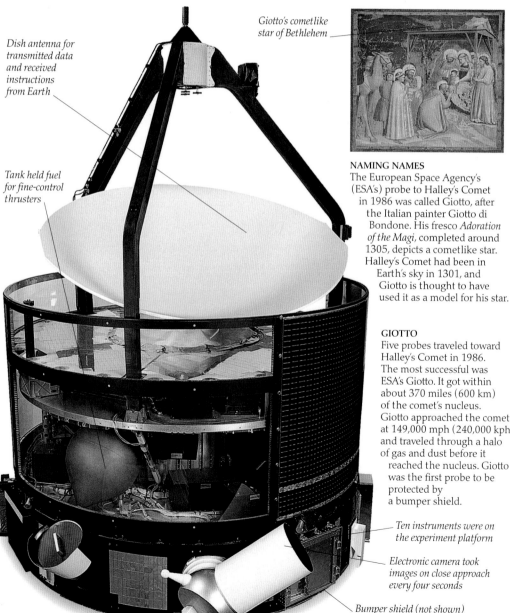

ON BOARD A SPACE PROBE are around 10 to 20 highly sensitive scientific instruments. These instruments of investigation record, monitor, and conduct experiments for Earth-based scientists. The information they supply enables astronomers and space scientists to build up a picture of the objects in space. The instruments are arguably the most important part of a space probe. They, however, rely on the main structure to transport, protect, and power them. Scientists often have to design instruments to work in unknown conditions and investigate objects previously viewed only from Earth. They may have to wait years before the instruments start to work and the results come in.

JOURNEY'S END
Space probes travel hundreds of millions of miles from Earth for years at a time. Most complete their journeys, but Mars-96, shown here, had a faulty booster rocket and failed to leave Earth's orbit.

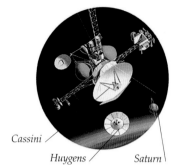

Cassini

Huygens   Saturn

SPACE PROBE TO SATURN
One of the most expensive and ambitious space probes to be built so far, Cassini reached Saturn in 2004 after a journey lasting nearly seven years. Cassini then started to orbit the planet and its moons before releasing a small probe, Huygens, which reached Titan, Saturn's largest moon, in January 2005. Cassini will continue to work until at least 2010.

Dish antenna for transmitted data and received instructions from Earth

Giotto's cometlike star of Bethlehem

Tank held fuel for fine-control thrusters

NAMING NAMES
The European Space Agency's (ESA's) probe to Halley's Comet in 1986 was called Giotto, after the Italian painter Giotto di Bondone. His fresco *Adoration of the Magi*, completed around 1305, depicts a cometlike star. Halley's Comet had been in Earth's sky in 1301, and Giotto is thought to have used it as a model for his star.

GIOTTO
Five probes traveled toward Halley's Comet in 1986. The most successful was ESA's Giotto. It got within about 370 miles (600 km) of the comet's nucleus. Giotto approached the comet at 149,000 mph (240,000 kph) and traveled through a halo of gas and dust before it reached the nucleus. Giotto was the first probe to be protected by a bumper shield.

Ten instruments were on the experiment platform

Electronic camera took images on close approach every four seconds

Bumper shield (not shown) attached here. This side of Giotto approached the comet

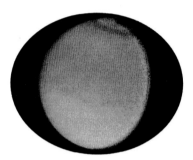

TITAN
Titan is shrouded by a thick, orange, nitrogen-rich atmosphere. The Huygens probe plunged through it, testing the atmosphere and measuring the windspeed as it fell. It touched down on the moon's surface on January 14, 2005, and sent back evidence of a thin, hard crust with softer material beneath.

TESTING HUYGENS
A heat shield protected Huygens as it dropped through Titan's upper atmosphere. This was then ejected, and the instruments set to work while parachutes controlled the probe's descent. A full-sized Huygens model was drop-tested on Earth (above) before launch.

HOW COLD?

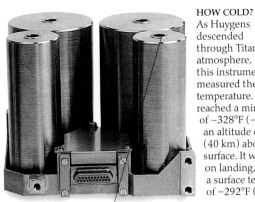

As Huygens descended through Titan's atmosphere, this instrument measured the temperature. It reached a minimum of −328°F (−200°C) at an altitude of 25 miles (40 km) above the surface. It warmed up on landing, registering a surface temperature of −292°F (−180°C).

Atmospheric gas flowed through the holes

DENSITY

This instrument was designed to measure the density of Titan's liquid ocean. But the probe hit dry land. We have subsequently discovered that most of Titan's hydrocarbon lakes and seas are near its polar regions.

FIRST TOUCH

This part of Huygens measured how quickly the probe stopped and what its landing site on Titan was like. The soil at the landing site was like loose wet sand. Its wetness was probably due to liquid methane, rather than water. Pebbles of hard water ice were scattered around.

Cable transfered data for storage then transmission

Transmitter received and sent "beeps"

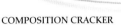

COMPOSITION CRACKER

By measuring the way a "beep" sound traveled between these two instruments, scientists found that Titan's atmosphere was 98.4 percent nitrogen and 1.6 percent methane. They also showed that the density near the surface was five times greater than the density of the air we breathe.

TOP-HAT SCIENCE

The five experiments in this top-hat sized piece of equipment, called the Surface Science Package (SSP), quantified the characteristics of Titan's lower atmosphere and surface. Until the craft arrived, scientists didn't know whether Huygens would hit land or ocean. We know now that the cold soil on this hilly satellite of Saturn is often saturated with methane, which evaporates to produce seasonal clouds and then methane rainfall.

Temperature and density instruments inside

Composition cracker

This part touched Titan's surface

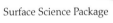

Surface Science Package

First touch

Ocean deep

Composition cracker

STAY COOL

Space technicians worked on Huygens at facilities in Bordeaux, France. They are installing the heat shield that will protect Huygens against high temperatures. The shield protected the craft from temperatures of up to 3,600°F (2,000°C), ensuring that the craft's inside temperature was kept far below 350°F (180°C).

DESCENT TO TITAN

Huygens took about 2 hours, 28 minutes to parachute down to the surface of Titan, and sent data for about 90 minutes after landing. The pressure at the surface was about 50 percent greater than that at the surface of Earth.

OCEAN DEEP

If Huygens had landed in an ocean, this instrument would have used sonar to measure its depth. Titan's lakes and seas are made up of the hydrocarbons methane and ethane in liquid form. The biggest lake is slightly larger than Earth's Caspian Sea.

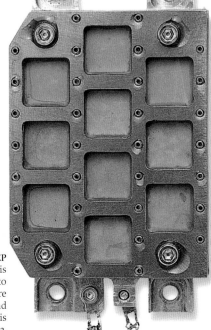

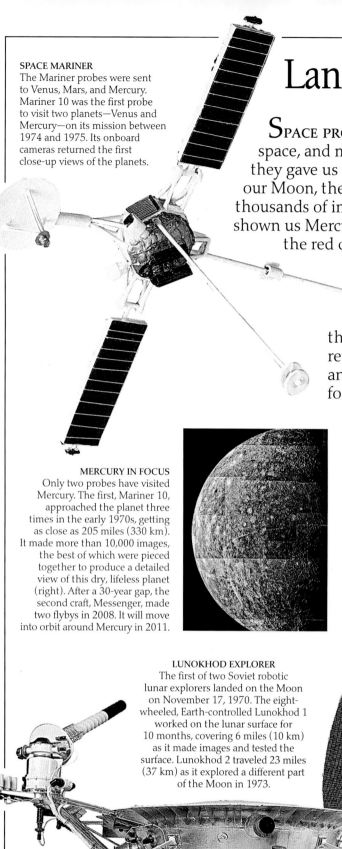

Landers and discoverers

SPACE PROBES ARE OUR EYES in space, and much more besides. Since they gave us the first detailed look at our Moon, they have made hundreds of thousands of images for us. They have shown us Mercury's cratered terrain, the red deserts of Mars, and the mountains and plains beneath the Venusian clouds. They have tested thick, hostile atmospheres, returned Moon rock to Earth, and searched Martian dust for signs of life. Probes follow preprogrammed instructions to investigate distant space objects for Earth-based scientists. They make discoveries that are expected, but also some that are not. Much of our knowledge about the solar system gained in the last four decades came from using probes, and the success of these space discoverers and landers means future missions are guaranteed.

VENUS REVEALED
The surface of Venus is hidden by its dense, hostile atmosphere. The first images of the planet's surface were sent by Venera craft in 1975. Since then, probes have mapped it with radar. This globe was made using radar images from Magellan in 1992.

MERCURY IN FOCUS
Only two probes have visited Mercury. The first, Mariner 10, approached the planet three times in the early 1970s, getting as close as 205 miles (330 km). It made more than 10,000 images, the best of which were pieced together to produce a detailed view of this dry, lifeless planet (right). After a 30-year gap, the second craft, Messenger, made two flybys in 2008. It will move into orbit around Mercury in 2011.

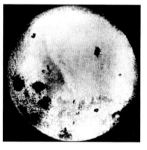

FAR SIDE OF THE MOON
The Moon has been studied from Earth for centuries, and, since 1959, US, Soviet, European, Japanese, Chinese, and Indian craft have visited it. Spacecraft show us what the side of the Moon facing away from Earth is like. The far side was first imaged by a Soviet probe on October 4, 1959.

LUNOKHOD EXPLORER
The first of two Soviet robotic lunar explorers landed on the Moon on November 17, 1970. The eight-wheeled, Earth-controlled Lunokhod 1 worked on the lunar surface for 10 months, covering 6 miles (10 km) as it made images and tested the surface. Lunokhod 2 traveled 23 miles (37 km) as it explored a different part of the Moon in 1973.

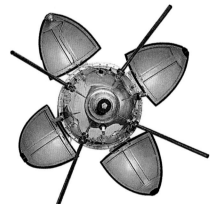

MOON DETECTIVES
The Soviet Luna series of space probes studied the Moon for almost 20 years. They were the first probes to travel to the Moon, to image the far side, to crash-land, and to orbit it. Luna 9 successfully achieved the first soft landing on February 3, 1966. It made the first panoramic pictures of the lunar surface, revealing details a fraction of an inch across.

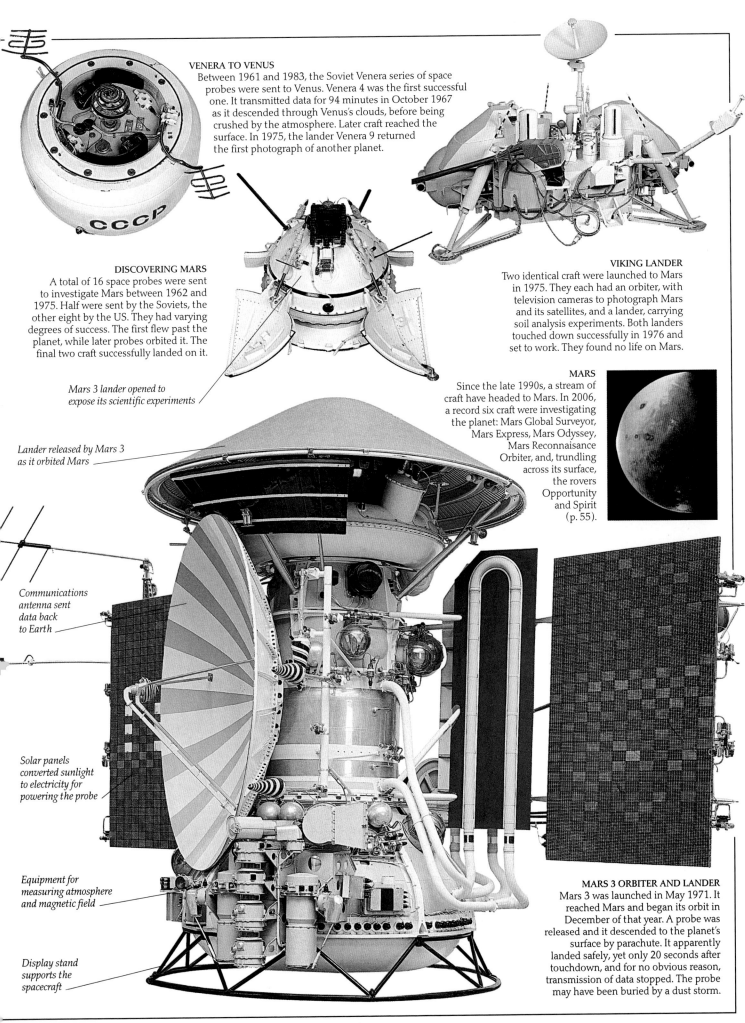

VENERA TO VENUS
Between 1961 and 1983, the Soviet Venera series of space probes were sent to Venus. Venera 4 was the first successful one. It transmitted data for 94 minutes in October 1967 as it descended through Venus's clouds, before being crushed by the atmosphere. Later craft reached the surface. In 1975, the lander Venera 9 returned the first photograph of another planet.

DISCOVERING MARS
A total of 16 space probes were sent to investigate Mars between 1962 and 1975. Half were sent by the Soviets, the other eight by the US. They had varying degrees of success. The first flew past the planet, while later probes orbited it. The final two craft successfully landed on it.

Mars 3 lander opened to expose its scientific experiments

Lander released by Mars 3 as it orbited Mars

Communications antenna sent data back to Earth

Solar panels converted sunlight to electricity for powering the probe

Equipment for measuring atmosphere and magnetic field

Display stand supports the spacecraft

VIKING LANDER
Two identical craft were launched to Mars in 1975. They each had an orbiter, with television cameras to photograph Mars and its satellites, and a lander, carrying soil analysis experiments. Both landers touched down successfully in 1976 and set to work. They found no life on Mars.

MARS
Since the late 1990s, a stream of craft have headed to Mars. In 2006, a record six craft were investigating the planet: Mars Global Surveyor, Mars Express, Mars Odyssey, Mars Reconnaisance Orbiter, and, trundling across its surface, the rovers Opportunity and Spirit (p. 55).

MARS 3 ORBITER AND LANDER
Mars 3 was launched in May 1971. It reached Mars and began its orbit in December of that year. A probe was released and it descended to the planet's surface by parachute. It apparently landed safely, yet only 20 seconds after touchdown, and for no obvious reason, transmission of data stopped. The probe may have been buried by a dust storm.

Crowded space

THE MOON IS EARTH'S ONLY NATURAL SATELLITE and its closest neighbor in space. In between is the virtual vacuum of space itself. But anyone visiting Earth for the first time might think that the volume of space immediately around Earth is crowded. Within a few thousand miles of its surface, there are about 1,000 operational satellites. Each one is a specialized scientific instrument following its own path around Earth. The satellites work for us in a variety of ways. Arguably, the most important are the telecommunications satellites that affect most of our lives. They give us global communications at the touch of a button, beam television pictures to our living rooms, and are used in all types of business, day and night.

TELSTAR
The first transatlantic live television pictures were transmitted in July 1962 by Telstar, a round, 35 in (90 cm) wide satellite covered in solar cells. In the years that followed, live television became an increasing part of life. By 1987, Roman Catholics on five continents could join Pope John Paul II in a live broadcast using 23 satellites.

Pocket-sized navigation systems can pinpoint your position to within a few yards

Terrorist at Munich Olympics, Germany

Opening ceremony of Beijing Olympics, China, 2008

GOOD NEWS, BAD NEWS
Satellites can turn a once local occasion into a real-time global experience in which billions of people can watch as events unfold. By 1972, at the Munich Olympic Games, terrorists had learned that live pictures can draw attention to their cause. In 2008, a TV audience of more than three billion worldwide saw the opening ceremony of the Beijing Olympic Games.

NAVIGATION
Aircraft pilots, yachtsmen, soldiers, and now hikers navigate their way around Earth using satellites. The Global Positioning System (GPS) uses a set of 31 satellites in orbit around Earth. The user sends a signal from a handset, like this one, which is received by up to 12 of the satellites. Return data give location, direction, and speed.

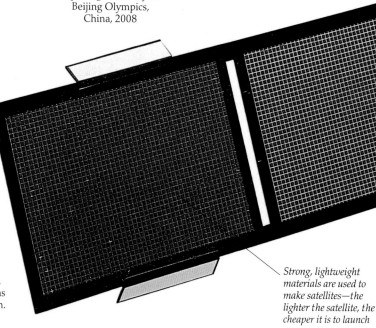

Strong, lightweight materials are used to make satellites—the lighter the satellite, the cheaper it is to launch

BUSY LINES
A telecommunications satellite has to handle tens of thousands of phone calls at once. In the 1980s, calls across Europe used the European Communications Satellite (ECS). ECS 1 was the first of five such satellites launched to provide 24 European countries with telephone services, television, and business links. Other areas of the world developed and used their own systems. Today, global systems exist. A series of satellites work together as they circle the world in a system known as a constellation.

GROUND CONTROL
Most satellites are launched by rocket, but some are taken into space in the payload bay of a space shuttle. Once the satellite has separated from the launcher, an onboard motor propels it into its correct orbit. Smaller maneuvers are made by the satellite's propulsion system throughout its lifetime to maintain its correct position and altitude in space. The rocket launch center now hands over to the satellite control center. They use ground stations, like this one in Belgium, to track the satellite, receive its signals, monitor its health, and send commands.

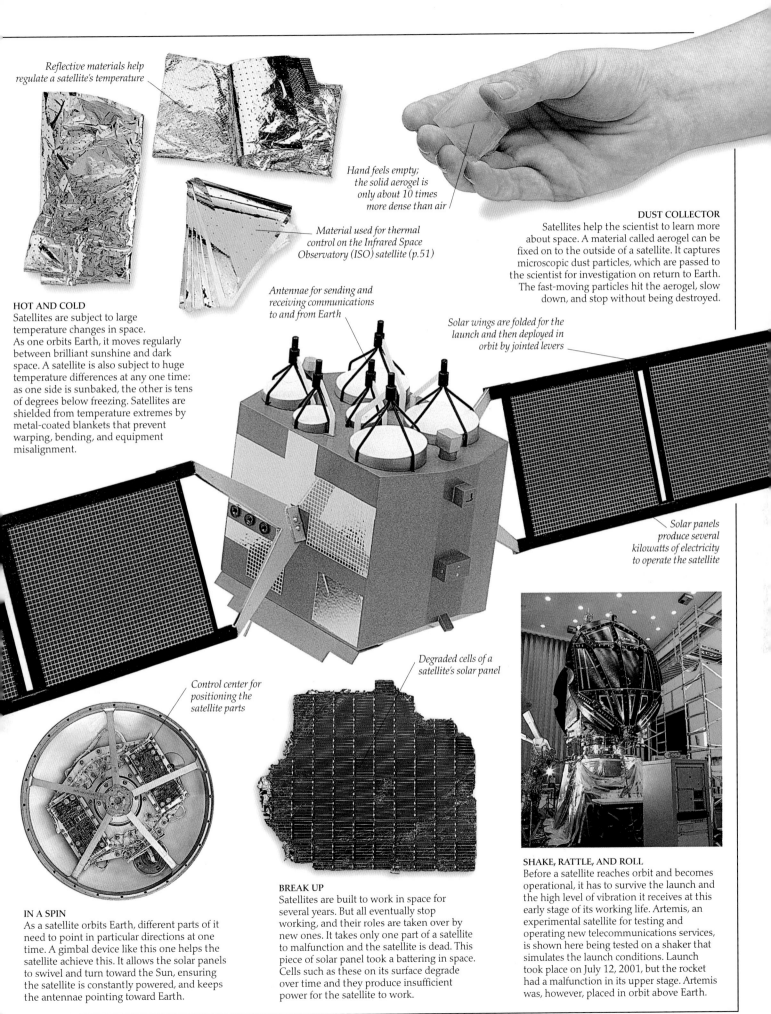

Reflective materials help regulate a satellite's temperature

Hand feels empty; the solid aerogel is only about 10 times more dense than air

Material used for thermal control on the Infrared Space Observatory (ISO) satellite (p.51)

DUST COLLECTOR
Satellites help the scientist to learn more about space. A material called aerogel can be fixed on to the outside of a satellite. It captures microscopic dust particles, which are passed to the scientist for investigation on return to Earth. The fast-moving particles hit the aerogel, slow down, and stop without being destroyed.

HOT AND COLD
Satellites are subject to large temperature changes in space. As one orbits Earth, it moves regularly between brilliant sunshine and dark space. A satellite is also subject to huge temperature differences at any one time: as one side is sunbaked, the other is tens of degrees below freezing. Satellites are shielded from temperature extremes by metal-coated blankets that prevent warping, bending, and equipment misalignment.

Antennae for sending and receiving communications to and from Earth

Solar wings are folded for the launch and then deployed in orbit by jointed levers

Solar panels produce several kilowatts of electricity to operate the satellite

Degraded cells of a satellite's solar panel

Control center for positioning the satellite parts

IN A SPIN
As a satellite orbits Earth, different parts of it need to point in particular directions at one time. A gimbal device like this one helps the satellite achieve this. It allows the solar panels to swivel and turn toward the Sun, ensuring the satellite is constantly powered, and keeps the antennae pointing toward Earth.

BREAK UP
Satellites are built to work in space for several years. But all eventually stop working, and their roles are taken over by new ones. It takes only one part of a satellite to malfunction and the satellite is dead. This piece of solar panel took a battering in space. Cells such as these on its surface degrade over time and they produce insufficient power for the satellite to work.

SHAKE, RATTLE, AND ROLL
Before a satellite reaches orbit and becomes operational, it has to survive the launch and the high level of vibration it receives at this early stage of its working life. Artemis, an experimental satellite for testing and operating new telecommunications services, is shown here being tested on a shaker that simulates the launch conditions. Launch took place on July 12, 2001, but the rocket had a malfunction in its upper stage. Artemis was, however, placed in orbit above Earth.

Looking at Earth

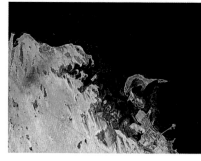

SATELLITES ARE CONTINUALLY TAKING a close look at our planet. In their different orbits around Earth they can survey the whole globe repeatedly or remain over one spot. Each one concentrates on collecting a specific type of information. Weather satellites look at clouds and study the Earth's atmosphere, or record the planet's range of surface temperatures. Both man-made structures and natural resources such as water, soil, and minerals, and flora and fauna, are mapped by others. Ocean currents, ice floes, and animal and bird movements are also followed. By taking time-lapse images of Earth, satellites are making records of short- and long-term planetary changes. The data they collect can be used to predict changes, and to avoid problems such as soil erosion and floods.

MAN-MADE DISASTER
The Landsat 5 satellite gives a bird's-eye view of a vast oil slick on the Saudi Arabian coast in 1991. False colors have been added to the image. The slick is colored rusty red. The oil had been deliberately released one month earlier by Iraqi soldiers in Kuwait.

Paris, France

FOUR CORNERS
The European Remote Sensing (ERS) satellites started work in 1991. ERS-1 made these four views of parts of Europe (above and in the other page corners) in 1992. Envisat, launched in 2002, is now the main European Earth-observing satellite. It collects information about our planet's land, water, ice, and atmosphere.

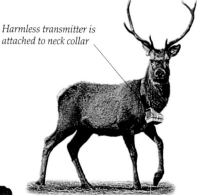

City of Detroit

Harmless transmitter is attached to neck collar

BIRD SPOTTING
The fish-eating Steller's sea eagle breeds in far eastern Russia. As winter approaches, the sea starts to freeze and the eagle's supply of food is cut off. Satellite tracking follows the birds as they fly south to spend the winter on the Japanese island of Hokkaido.

DEERSTALKER
Transmitters are sometimes attached to animals, such as this red deer. As the deer moves around, a signal is released that is picked up by satellite. Over time, its habitual movements are revealed. By knowing where animals breed, feed, and spend winter, conservationists can protect such sites and so conserve the creatures.

Geometrically shaped man-made fields stand out

EYE IN THE SKY
The French Earth observation satellite, Spot-1, was launched in 1986. Every 26 days, it photographed the whole of Earth's surface. On board were two telescopes, each observing a 37 mile (60 km) wide strip of land below the satellite. Objects only 3 ft (10 m) across were recorded. This Spot-1 picture of farmland in Canada was made in July 1988. False colors identify different crops at different stages of growth. Lake St Clair, at the top of the picture, and Lake Erie, at the bottom, both appear black.

London, England

MAN ON THE MOVE
Air-, sea-, and land-based forces all use satellite systems. Their planes and ships carry equipment that can receive signals from navigation satellites. For a lone soldier in remote terrain, such as desert, a navigation backpack is the answer. It tells him where he is and in which direction to move. A portable communications system keeps him in touch with other troops.

Portable folding satellite dish

Vienna, Austria

Solar cells supply energy for Meteosat to function

Upper platform carries communications equipment

WEATHER WATCH
Meteosat weather satellites have been in operation since 1977. They are are in geostationary orbit, which means their orbit is synchronized with Earth's rotation, so they stay above a particular spot on Earth and monitor the same region. Data from these and other satellites are combined to study global weather patterns and used to make daily forecasts.

ERUPTION
Images of natural phenomena, such as volcanoes, are made by satellites and by astronaut-operated equipment on board their craft. Smoke and ash from an active volcano can be monitored and aircraft warned away. Ground movements of a few inches to several yards that may warn of a volcanic eruption, can be detected and the alarm raised.

LOOK AND LEARN
Events and places on Earth can be watched by people thousands of miles away because of communications satellites. People can learn about different nations and cultures from their own homes. In 1975, over 2,400 villages in India were given satellite dishes and televisions. Direct broadcasting by satellite instructed them on hygiene and health, family planning, and farming methods.

Zeeland, the Netherlands

Looking into space

SCIENTIFIC SATELLITES ARE USED BY ASTRONOMERS to look away from the Earth and into space. They are telescopes that collect and record data in much the same way that telescopes do on Earth. But from their vantage point, they can study the universe 24 hours a day, 365 days a year. Space telescopes operate in a range of wavelengths. Much of the information they collect, such as that at X-ray wavelengths, would be stopped from reaching ground-based instruments by Earth's atmosphere. Data collected by telescopes working in optical, X-ray, infrared, ultraviolet, microwave, and other wavelengths are combined to make a more complete view of space. This data is collected, stored, and sent to a ground station, where it is decoded by computers. Astronomers all over the world have been looking at the universe in this way for about 40 years.

EARLY ASTRONOMY
Astronomers once recorded their findings in drawings, like this one. Today, electronic devices record data transmitted from telescopes in Earth's orbit.

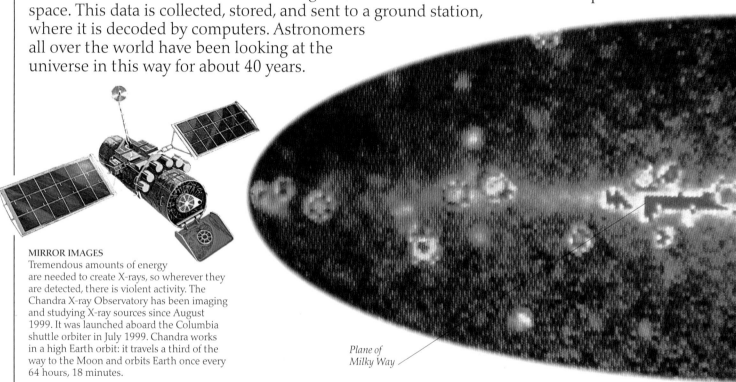

MIRROR IMAGES
Tremendous amounts of energy are needed to create X-rays, so wherever they are detected, there is violent activity. The Chandra X-ray Observatory has been imaging and studying X-ray sources since August 1999. It was launched aboard the Columbia shuttle orbiter in July 1999. Chandra works in a high Earth orbit: it travels a third of the way to the Moon and orbits Earth once every 64 hours, 18 minutes.

Plane of Milky Way

OUR GALACTIC CENTER
The High Energy Astrophysics Observatory X-ray satellite telescope took this false-color X-ray view of our galaxy. The view covers two-thirds of Earth's sky. The plane of the Milky Way crosses the center of the picture from left to right. The black, then red, areas are the most intense X-ray emitters. The yellow and green areas emit less X-ray energy, and the blue areas the least.

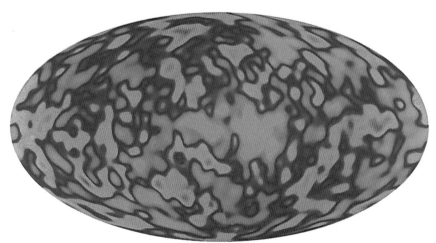

RIPPLES IN THE SKY
In 1992, the Cosmic Background Explorer (COBE) satellite discovered slight temperature differences in the universe's microwave background radiation. In this false-color microwave map of the whole sky, the average temperature of the background radiation is shown as deep blue. The pink and red areas are warmer, and the pale blue cooler. These were the ripples scientists predicted should exist in background radiation created by the Big Bang (see right).

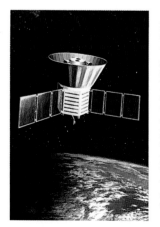

MICROWAVE IMAGES
COBE, the first satellite telescope to look at space in the microwave region, was launched by rocket into an orbit about 570 miles (920 km) above Earth. COBE started work in late 1989. It provided the first observational proof for the theory that the universe was created in a huge explosion we call the Big Bang about 13.7 billion years ago.

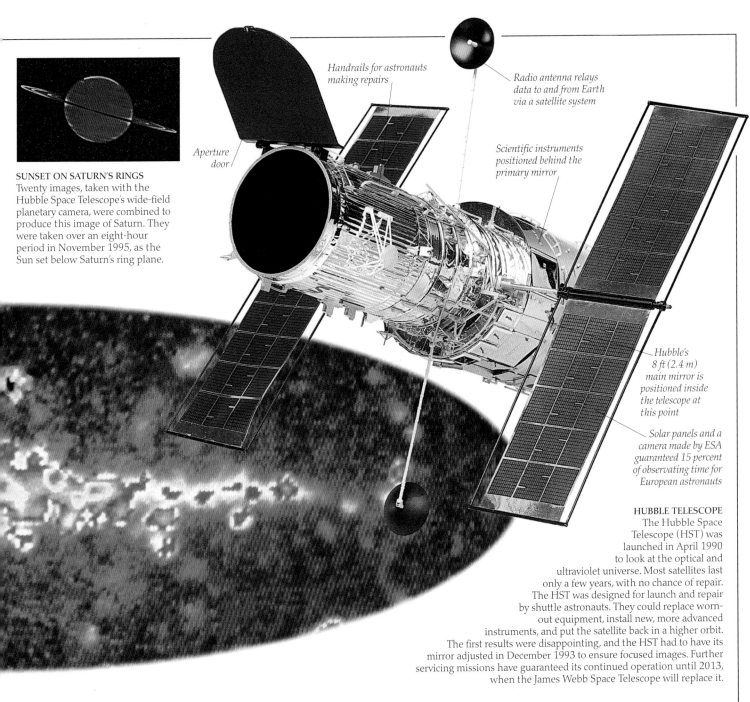

SUNSET ON SATURN'S RINGS
Twenty images, taken with the Hubble Space Telescope's wide-field planetary camera, were combined to produce this image of Saturn. They were taken over an eight-hour period in November 1995, as the Sun set below Saturn's ring plane.

Handrails for astronauts making repairs

Aperture door

Radio antenna relays data to and from Earth via a satellite system

Scientific instruments positioned behind the primary mirror

Hubble's 8 ft (2.4 m) main mirror is positioned inside the telescope at this point

Solar panels and a camera made by ESA guaranteed 15 percent of observating time for European astronauts

HUBBLE TELESCOPE
The Hubble Space Telescope (HST) was launched in April 1990 to look at the optical and ultraviolet universe. Most satellites last only a few years, with no chance of repair. The HST was designed for launch and repair by shuttle astronauts. They could replace worn-out equipment, install new, more advanced instruments, and put the satellite back in a higher orbit. The first results were disappointing, and the HST had to have its mirror adjusted in December 1993 to ensure focused images. Further servicing missions have guaranteed its continued operation until 2013, when the James Webb Space Telescope will replace it.

ISO being tested by ESA, before launch in 1995

Launch of ISO by Ariane 4, November 1995

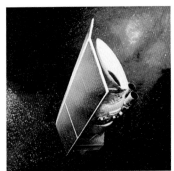

Artist's impression of ISO in orbit

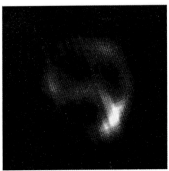

Picture taken by ISO of a supernova, or an exploding star

INFRARED OBSERVATIONS
The European Space Agency's (ESA's) Infrared Space Observatory (ISO) made 26,000 scientific observations in its working lifetime, from 1995 to 1998. From its elliptical orbit, which took it from 600 miles (1,000 km) to 43,500 miles (70,000 km) above the Earth, ISO used its 2 ft (60 cm) mirror to observe the near and distant universe, making on average 45 observations a day. Data on materials in Saturn, the birth of stars, colliding galaxies, and water ice in our galaxy were all sent to the ESA's tracking station in Madrid, Spain.

Spin-offs

SPACE INDUSTRY RESEARCH is used to benefit our everyday lives. Many technologies and techniques designed for use in space have been transferred or adapted for life on Earth, often in fields totally unrelated to the original research. An everyday item such as food wrapping was developed from reflective film used on satellites. Car control systems used by one-handed drivers came from the one-handed technique used in the Lunar Rover, and modern smoke detection systems use technology developed for smoke detection on the Skylab space station. Tens of thousands of spin-offs have come from space research, many of which have been adapted for medical use.

LASER BEAM
Robot and laser technology developed for space is used in equipment for people with disabilities. The boy above, who is unable to speak, is wearing a headpiece with laser equipment. By using the laser beam to operate a voice synthesizer, he is able to communicate.

INSULIN PUMP
Robert Fischell, an American space scientist, invented an insulin pump for diabetics. Once implanted in the body, the device automatically delivers precise preprogrammed amounts of insulin. The pumping mechanism is based on technology used by the Viking craft that landed on the planet Mars in 1976.

KEEPING CLEAN
An industrial cleaning method that is quick, easy to use, and harmless to the environment has grown out of space research. Ricelike pellets of dry ice (solid carbon dioxide) are blasted at a surface at supersonic speeds to remove dirt. On impact, the ice turns to gas, the dirt falls away, and the underlying material is unharmed.

Silver kidskin outfit

Artificial hand and control system

SPACE ON THE SLOPES
Protective clothing designed for astronauts is now used on the ski slopes. The Apollo helmet design, which gave the astronauts fog-free sight, has been adapted for use in ski goggles. Electrically heated or fan-controlled goggles prevent moisture from condensing inside, so that the goggles do not fog up.

Mercury astronauts

THE SPACE LOOK
The first US astronauts, on the Mercury rockets, wore silver suits designed to reflect heat. The space look was transferred to haute couture when French fashion designer André Courrèges produced his space-age style collection in 1964. Within months, off-the-rack, space-influenced fashions were available to everyone.

HAND CONTROL
The micro-miniaturization of parts for space has been adapted for use on Earth. Artificial limbs with controls as small as coins have been developed. This makes the limbs lighter and easier to use. Devices that are no larger than a pinhead and can be placed in a human heart to monitor its rhythm are another space technology spin-off.

Patient enters a body scanner to have the body imaged

SHARP VIEW
An image-enhancement technique devised to improve the sharpness of Moon photographs is used in medical photography. It gives doctors a better basis for diagnosis by providing more accurate images. Body scanners give a much clearer overall view of what is happening inside the human body.

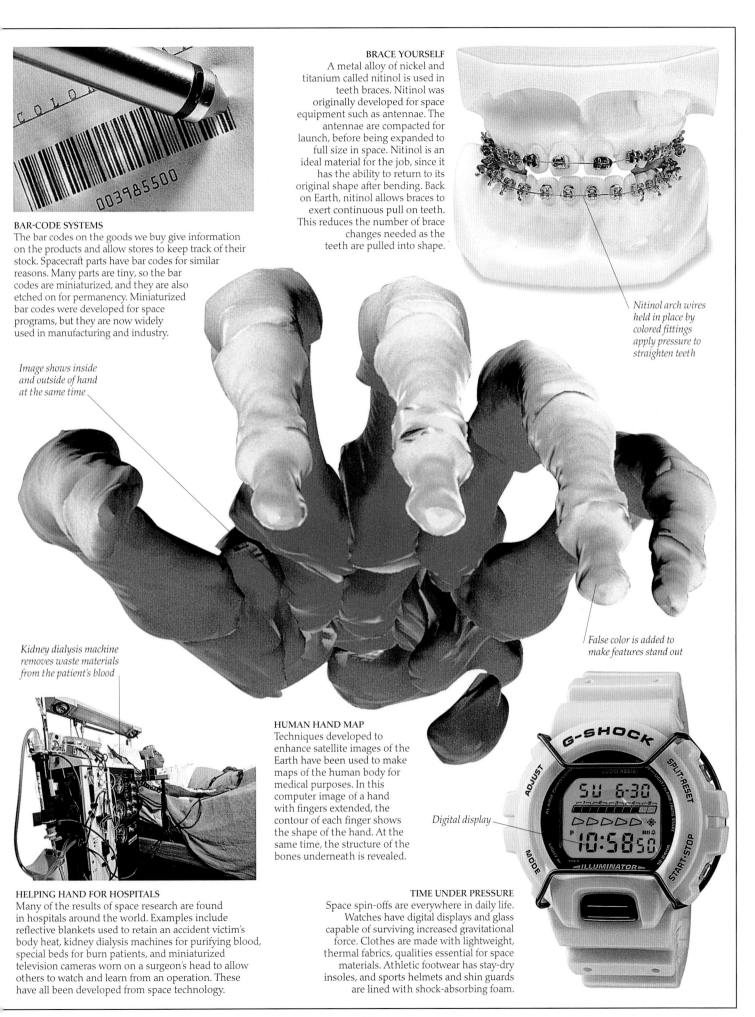

BAR-CODE SYSTEMS
The bar codes on the goods we buy give information on the products and allow stores to keep track of their stock. Spacecraft parts have bar codes for similar reasons. Many parts are tiny, so the bar codes are miniaturized, and they are also etched on for permanency. Miniaturized bar codes were developed for space programs, but they are now widely used in manufacturing and industry.

BRACE YOURSELF
A metal alloy of nickel and titanium called nitinol is used in teeth braces. Nitinol was originally developed for space equipment such as antennae. The antennae are compacted for launch, before being expanded to full size in space. Nitinol is an ideal material for the job, since it has the ability to return to its original shape after bending. Back on Earth, nitinol allows braces to exert continuous pull on teeth. This reduces the number of brace changes needed as the teeth are pulled into shape.

Nitinol arch wires held in place by colored fittings apply pressure to straighten teeth

Image shows inside and outside of hand at the same time

Kidney dialysis machine removes waste materials from the patient's blood

False color is added to make features stand out

HUMAN HAND MAP
Techniques developed to enhance satellite images of the Earth have been used to make maps of the human body for medical purposes. In this computer image of a hand with fingers extended, the contour of each finger shows the shape of the hand. At the same time, the structure of the bones underneath is revealed.

Digital display

HELPING HAND FOR HOSPITALS
Many of the results of space research are found in hospitals around the world. Examples include reflective blankets used to retain an accident victim's body heat, kidney dialysis machines for purifying blood, special beds for burn patients, and miniaturized television cameras worn on a surgeon's head to allow others to watch and learn from an operation. These have all been developed from space technology.

TIME UNDER PRESSURE
Space spin-offs are everywhere in daily life. Watches have digital displays and glass capable of surviving increased gravitational force. Clothes are made with lightweight, thermal fabrics, qualities essential for space materials. Athletic footwear has stay-dry insoles, and sports helmets and shin guards are lined with shock-absorbing foam.

21st-century exploration

SINCE THE SPACE AGE BEGAN over 50 years ago, we have learned an enormous amount about the universe. The learning continues as the 21st century unfolds. Robotic probes are returning to worlds already seen first-hand and investigating others for the first time. New satellites replace craft that have served us well. While some continue to give us a global perspective of our home planet, others look into deep space and reveal even more of the universe.

EARLY SUCCESS

The Near Earth Asteroid Rendezvous (NEAR) space probe was one of the first successes of the 21st century. NEAR left for the asteroid belt in 1996. It reached its target, the asteroid Eros, and on February 14, 2000, began to orbit it. On February 12, 2001, scientists changed NEAR's flight plan and landed the probe on the asteroid—another first.

COST CUTTER

Some late-1990s space probes were designed to be faster and cheaper than earlier probes and still bring better results. The success of two such probes, Pathfinder to Mars and NEAR to Eros, has meant this approach continues in the 21st century. StarDust (right), launched in 1999, kept its costs down by taking seven years to complete a round-trip to Comet Wild-2. In January 2006, it returned to Earth with the first particles collected from any comet.

StarDust

The main mirror for collecting infrared waves is 11 ft 6 in (3.5 m) across

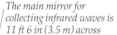

Herschel Space Observatory

SCIENCE SATELLITES

The Herschel Space Observatory is one of a group of science satellites gathering data in the early decades of the 21st century. From late 2009, its mirror will collect long-wavelength infrared radiation from some of the universe's coolest and most distant objects. A second mission, Planck, launched with Herschel but operating independently, will study the cosmic microwave background radiation—the dying heat of the Big Bang (see p. 50).

TESTING TIME

New technologies are constantly being developed for use in spacecraft. They undergo long and extensive testing before use. A failure in space could mean the end of an otherwise successful mission. The probe Deep Space 1 tested 12 new technologies during its three-year mission to asteroid Braille and Comet Borelly. It tested a new form of engine (the ion-propulsion engine), a miniature camera, and computer software that let a craft think and act on its own. The mission was part of the US's New Millennium program, designed to speed up space exploration by testing advanced technologies in space itself.

Deep Space 1 being launched by Delta rocket in October 1998

MESSENGER TO MERCURY

Launched in 2004, Messenger first encountered Mercury in January 2008. It made a second flyby in October 2008. After a third in December 2009, Messenger will return to start a year-long orbit of the planet in 2011. Its instruments are designed to work in the extreme environment near the Sun. They will image all of Mercury for the first time, and gather data on the planet's composition, structure, and geological past.

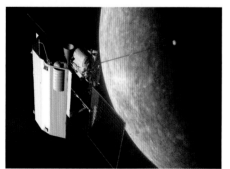

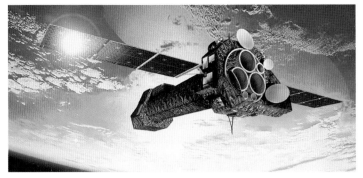

EYE ON SPACE

The X-ray Multi-Mirror Mission (XMM-Newton) is the most powerful orbiting X-ray telescope. Launched by the European Space Agency (ESA) in December 1999, its mission will last until 2012. It is detecting more X-ray sources than any previous satellite and is helping us understand black holes and the early universe.

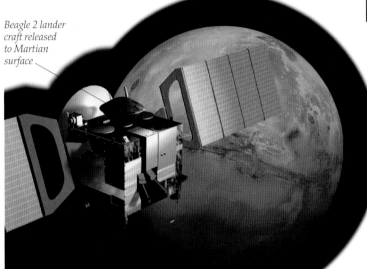

Beagle 2 lander craft released to Martian surface

MARS EXPRESS

Mars Express moved into orbit around Mars on December 25, 2003. It was Europe's first planetary mission. From early 2004, its instruments have been imaging Mars's surface, mapping its mineral composition, and studying the Martian atmosphere. It has uncovered evidence of a watery landscape in the planet's past. On arrival at Mars, it released the lander Beagle 2 to journey to the surface, but contact with the lander was lost.

EYE ON EARTH

Envisat is the largest and most advanced Earth observation satellite ever built in Europe. It is the size of semitrailer truck and has been orbiting Earth 14 times a day since March 2002. Its 10 instruments monitor our planet and can detect natural or man-made changes on land, in water, or in the air. In its 10-year lifetime, it will send one million PCs-worth of data back to the European Space Agency's ground station in Sweden.

The Genesis spacecraft with its conical reentry shield undergoing prelaunch preparations

Space engineers wear protective clothing and work in the Cleanroom to avoid contaminating the craft with human or Earth dust

A pair of cameras called Pancam take panoramic views

Antenna communicates directly with Earth, or via a craft orbiting Mars

ROBOT GEOLOGISTS

Two identical vehicles, Spirit and Opportunity, have been roving over opposite sides of the planet Mars since January 2004. They travel at about 2 in (5 cm) per second looking for signs of past water activity. These robot geologists occasionally stop to make on-the-spot investigations. An articulated arm at the front places instruments directly up against the rock and soil. Its mechanical fist contains a camera, as well as a tool to expose the inside of rocks.

SAMPLE RETURN

The Genesis mission, launched on August 8, 2001, collected material from the Sun and returned it to Earth. After orbiting the Sun for two years, Genesis returned with solar wind particles—material flowing out from the Sun. Scientists are comparing the composition of these particles with that of the planets to learn more about the way the Sun and the planets formed from a cloud of gas and dust some 4.6 billion years ago.

International Space Station

AT THE DAWN OF THE SPACE AGE, in the late 1950s, only a handful of countries were working to get into space. Just two, the United States and the Soviet Union, had the know-how and the money to succeed, and they worked in isolation to outdo one another. Today, countries pool knowledge and resources to build and launch satellites and space probes. The old rivals, the US and Russia, have joined with more than 10 other nations to build the International Space Station (ISS), a workplace in space visited by astronauts from across the globe.

FIRST CREW
On November 2, 2000, the first crew to live on the ISS moved in. They were Yuri Gidzenko, William Shepherd, and Sergei Krikalev (left to right). They arrived on a Soyuz craft but left by space shuttle 138 days later. The three are from the US and Russia, but the ISS has also been home to crews from 16 nations and six space tourists.

CONSTRUCTING THE INTERNATIONAL SPACE STATION
The ISS is being assembled in space. Construction started in December 1998, and it is scheduled for completion in 2011. Over 100 parts, delivered in more than 50 launches, are fixed together by astronauts on more than 100 space walks. The ISS came alive when James Newman (below) and Jerry Ross linked and powered up the first two modules, Zarya and Unity.

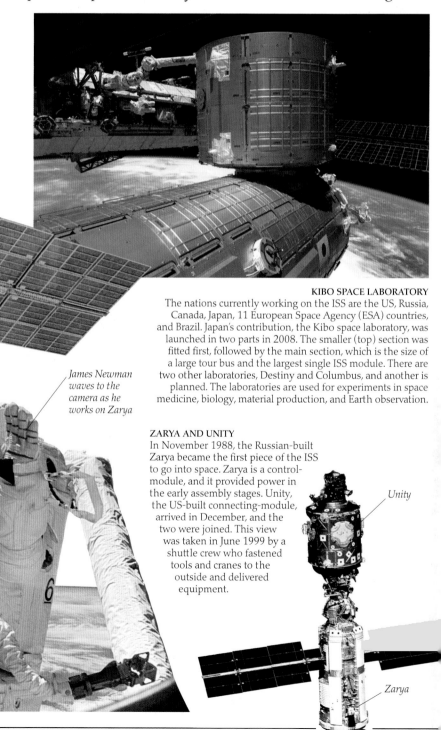

The Endeavour orbiter is reflected in Newman's visor

James Newman waves to the camera as he works on Zarya

KIBO SPACE LABORATORY
The nations currently working on the ISS are the US, Russia, Canada, Japan, 11 European Space Agency (ESA) countries, and Brazil. Japan's contribution, the Kibo space laboratory, was launched in two parts in 2008. The smaller (top) section was fitted first, followed by the main section, which is the size of a large tour bus and the largest single ISS module. There are two other laboratories, Destiny and Columbus, and another is planned. The laboratories are used for experiments in space medicine, biology, material production, and Earth observation.

ZARYA AND UNITY
In November 1988, the Russian-built Zarya became the first piece of the ISS to go into space. Zarya is a control-module, and it provided power in the early assembly stages. Unity, the US-built connecting-module, arrived in December, and the two were joined. This view was taken in June 1999 by a shuttle crew who fastened tools and cranes to the outside and delivered equipment.

Unity

Zarya

NEARING COMPLETION
The ISS is a bit bigger than a football field. It orbits Earth at 17,500 mph (28,000 kph) and at an altitude of 240 miles (390 km). This view, taken in June 2008, was recorded from the space shuttle Discovery as it moved away from the station. Discovery had delivered the Japanese-built Kibo space laboratory. The Kibo module was the station's 18th major component, leaving only three major parts to be added before the ISS's scheduled completion in late 2011.

Columbus laboratory module holds 10 racks of experiments, each the size of a phone booth

Kibo module was so large it barely fit into Discovery's payload bay

Jules Verne ATV docked with the ISS from April to September 2008

CREW TRANSPORTATION
Astronauts are ferried to and from the ISS inside a Russian Soyuz capsule, or on board a US space shuttle. The capsule is launched by a Soyuz rocket. Once in orbit, the capsule spends two days chasing the ISS before docking with it. When the air pressure between the two craft has been equalized, the hatches open and the crew enter the station. Returning crew travel back to Earth in the capsule; they land less than three and a half hours after leaving the ISS.

Soyuz capsule with three crew is launched to the ISS from Baikonur, Kazakhstan

SUPPLY CRAFT
Progress is an uncrewed, automated Russian craft that, along with the European Automated Transfer Vehicle (ATV), takes supplies to the ISS. Progress is launched by Soyuz rocket and usually docks with the Zvezda service module. The ISS crew unload the supplies, then fill the craft with waste and unwanted equipment, which burn up with Progress as it reenters the Earth's atmosphere.

UNDER CONTROL
Guests and officials in the Space Mission Control Center in Korolyov, Russia, watch as members of the 16th and 17th ISS crews broadcast from their space home in April 2008. The astronauts seen on the Control Center screen include Peggy Whitson, who had just completed a six-month stay on the station and was about to return home.

The way ahead

SPACE SCIENTISTS ARE ALWAYS looking ahead. As one group works on missions to be launched in the next few years, another plans craft and journeys for future decades. They predict that by the mid-21st century, astronauts will have returned to the Moon, and the first crew will have traveled to a new destination—the planet Mars. Meanwhile, astronauts will continue to live and work on space stations, and robotic craft will study new targets. If the search for Earth-like planets is successful, a whole new area of investigation may open up. Space travel could become as familiar in the years ahead as air travel is today. Commercial space planes will give private individuals the chance to travel away from the Earth and experience space for themselves.

CHINA IN SPACE
Astronaut Zhai Zhigang waves his nation's flag during a 15-minute space walk in September 2008. It was China's first space walk, and a key stage in the nation's developing space industry. When China launched its first astronaut in October 2003, it became only the third country to take people into space. China intends to build a space station, but it also has its eye on the Moon: it sent a probe there in 2007, and further expeditions are expected.

THE NEXT MILLENNIUM
Predicting the future is not easy. Only 50 years ago, it was thought that space travel, shown here in the film *2001: A Space Odyssey*, would be a regular part of early 21st-century life. Predictions for 3001 include a ring-shaped star city orbiting above Earth's equator. Future generations will reach it by a space lift directly linking the city with our planet.

Artist's impression of the sailcraft

SAILCRAFT
Scientists are investigating forms of propulsion that could take craft to the edge of the solar system and on toward the stars. One approach is to sail across space without the need of an engine, or fuel. The craft in this artwork, known as the sailcraft, has wafer-thin sails. The accumulative pressure of sunlight on the sails would propel the craft on its journey.

ORION CREW VEHICLE
This artist's impression shows the Orion spacecraft on its way to the International Space Station (ISS). Orion, which will take over the space shuttle's role of carrying crew and cargo to the station, is scheduled to make its first journey there in 2014. At a future date, the craft will carry astronauts to the Moon. A separate module will undock from Orion and carry the crew to the lunar surface. Meanwhile, Orion will wait in lunar orbit for up to six months before returning the astronauts home.

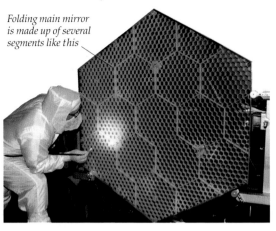

Folding main mirror is made up of several segments like this

COMET CHASER
The Rosetta spacecraft is one of the most ambitious space missions ever attempted. After a 10-year journey, Rosetta will arrive at Comet Churyumov-Gerasimenko in May 2014. The craft will release a small lander named Philae on to the comet's surface, before moving into orbit around the comet. Rosetta will travel with the comet for the next two years, monitoring changes as it heads toward the Sun.

SPACE TELESCOPE
A mirror segment of the James Webb Space Telescope, the successor to the Hubble Space Telescope, is prepared for a 2013 launch. The Webb Telescope is much larger than Hubble, works in infrared (Hubble is a visible-light telescope), and has an innovative folding main mirror. Webb will make observations while stationed 900,000 miles (1.5 million km) from Earth.

SpaceShipOne is just 28 ft long (8.5 m)

Rocket motor propels craft to edge of space

ANYONE THERE?
The Kepler spacecraft started its mission—to look for Earth-like planets—aboard a Delta II rocket in March 2009. It then moved into position, trailing our planet as we orbit the Sun. Kepler points at a patch of sky containing about 4.5 million detectable stars, but it is only interested in 100,000 of them. These are all Sun-like stars that may have Earth-like planets. If any such planets are found, we may be one step closer to finding extraterrestrial life.

SPACE TOURISM
Until recently, the only way to go into space was to enrol as an astronaut with a national space agency and be launched by Russia, the US, or China. Since 2001, space tourists have paid to stay on the ISS, and soon it will be possible to travel with a commercial organization. In 2004, SpaceShipOne, the first privately designed and owned spacecraft, completed its first flight. Seats at $200,000 each are now being booked for 60 mile (100 km) high, nonorbital trips in around 2010.

NEXT STOP MARS
There are plans to send astronauts to Mars, but this will not be until the mid-2030s. The US's Orion (see far left) will ferry crews to spacecraft assembled above Earth, and these will then journey on to Mars. A round trip would take about a year and a half if the astronauts spent just three weeks on the planet. If they stayed any longer, they would have to wait for Earth and Mars to realign before returning home, making a round trip of about three years.

Did you know?

FASCINATING FACTS

Victory for solar car Nuna

Space technology can be used to improve designs on Earth. In 2001, a Dutch solar car called Nuna, developed using European space technology, won the World Solar Challenge. Nuna completed the 1,870-mile (3,010-km) race across Australia in just 32 hours, 39 minutes.

On July 31, 1999, eminent geologist Gene Shoemaker became the first person to be "buried" on the Moon. His ashes were aboard Lunar Prospector when it was launched on January 6, 1998. The craft circled the Moon for 18 months and then crash-landed onto the surface.

Experiment to test the effects of weightlessness

There are plans to send astronauts on longer missions farther into space in the future. To prepare for this, scientists are investigating the long-term effects on the human body of living without gravity. One experiment involved getting volunteers to lie at an angle of 6° (a position that simulates many of the effects of weightlessness) nonstop for three months.

A shuttle orbiter uses 8,500–10,000 ft (2,600–3,000 m) of runway from touchdown to wheel stop, compared to around 3,000–4,000 ft (900–1,200 m) used by a commercial airliner.

About five minutes before touchdown, a shuttle orbiter makes two sonic booms. The first is generated by the nose, and it is followed rapidly by the second, generated by the wings.

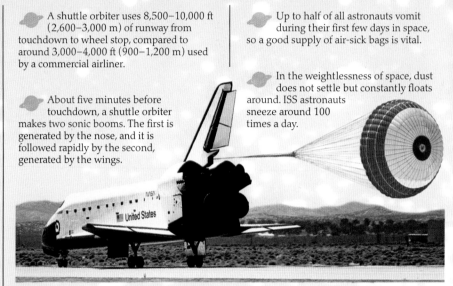

The drag chute slows down the space shuttle orbiter as it lands

By the start of 2009, the shuttle fleet had notched up 131 flights, completing over 18,500 orbits of Earth. Discovery made the most flights, a total of 37. Between them the fleet docked to the International Space Station (ISS) 23 times. Nine more flights are scheduled before the fleet retires in 2010.

NASA stayed in touch with Pioneer 10, the probe launched for Jupiter in 1972, for over 30 years. It was built for a 21-month mission, but its last signal was received in January 2003. The signal took more than 11 hours to travel the 7.6 billion miles (12.2 billion km) to Earth.

When the Pathfinder probe landed on Mars in 1997, it was inside a giant ball of airbags for protection. The probe bounced 15 times on the surface, then rolled to a stop and the airbags deflated. The three panels of the probe then opened to expose the instruments and to allow the Sojourner Rover to take off down the ramp and explore the surface of Mars.

Up to half of all astronauts vomit during their first few days in space, so a good supply of air-sick bags is vital.

In the weightlessness of space, dust does not settle but constantly floats around. ISS astronauts sneeze around 100 times a day.

The European Space Agency held a competition to name the four Cluster satellites that were launched in 2000 to study the interaction between the Sun and the Earth's magnetic field. The winner chose the names of four dances—Tango, Salsa, Samba, and Rumba—because the satellites would be dancing in formation in space.

The Hubble Space Telescope cannot afford to suffer from camera-shake. Its incredible instruments can lock onto a subject and hold still, deviating less than the width that a human hair would appear from 1 mile (1.6 km) away.

In 1966, Eugene Cernan, from Gemini IX, did a space walk of 2 hours, 7 minutes, beating the previous record of 36 minutes. During this time, the craft had orbited Earth so Cernan has the honor of being the first man to walk around the world. This was a tough task in itself, but Cernan then had trouble getting into the craft and closing the hatch. When he took off his suit, he emptied almost 2 pints (1 liter) of sweat from his boots.

View of Martian landscape from Pathfinder

The solar panels of Pathfinder

Ramp

Sojourner Rover next to rock nicknamed Yogi

Deflated airbag

New Horizons probe to Pluto

Q Are there any plans to send a probe to Pluto? How long would it take to get there?

A The New Horizons spacecraft is already on its way to Pluto. It was launched in January 2006 and will arrive at the dwarf planet in July 2015. On board are seven instruments, including a camera to collect data as it flys by Pluto and its three moons. After mapping Pluto, New Horizons will head into the Kuiper Belt to look at one or more of its icy objects.

Q What sort of temperatures occur in space? Is it hot or cold?

A The temperature on Earth ranges from −94 to 131°F (−70 to 55°C), but in space, temperatures range between −150 and 250°F (−101 and 121°C). The temperature depends on whether you are in sunlight or in shadow.

Q What caused the Challenger and Columbia space shuttle disasters?

A The day of the Challenger launch in 1986 was extremely cold, and this affected a seal on one of the solid rocket boosters. Fuel escaped and ignited 73 seconds after launch, blowing the shuttle apart. Shuttle flights were suspended for two years while safety was reviewed. The 2003 disintegration of Columbia was caused by hot gas entering the shuttle's wing through a hole. The hole had been made at launch 16 days earlier by a piece of foam that peeled off the fuel tank.

Q When will people other than astronauts be able to travel in space?

A They already can—if they have a lot of money. In April 2001, California millionaire Dennis Tito became the first space tourist when he paid around $20 million for an eight-day trip to the International Space Station (ISS). Tito enjoyed the experience and said, "I was worried that I might not feel good in space. I turned out to feel the best I've felt in my entire life."

Q Is life in space almost completely silent? Is it quiet in a spacecraft, too?

A Astronauts experience extremes of noise and silence. Space is silent because there is no air through which sound can travel. On an extra-vehicular activity (EVA), astronauts cannot hear each other, even if they are side by side. They communicate by radio. But air is pumped inside a spacecraft, and life inside is very noisy. A launch is louder still— a hundred million times louder than a normal conversation!

Pieces of Mir blaze through the Earth's atmosphere

Q What happened when the space station Mir was abandoned?

A On March 23, 2001, after 86,320 orbits, Russian Mission Control fired engines to knock Mir out of orbit and into the Earth's atmosphere, where it broke up. This could be seen from Earth, as the picture above, taken from Fiji in the South Pacific, shows. Some pieces burned up in the atmosphere, but larger parts landed in the Pacific Ocean between Chile and New Zealand.

Space tourist
Dennis Tito

Record breakers

LONGEST SINGLE STAY IN SPACE
On March 22, 1995, Russian cosmonaut Valeri Poliakov returned to Earth after 438 days, 17 hours, 58 minutes, and 16 seconds in space.

MOST TIME SPENT IN SPACE
Sergei Krikalev holds the record for the total time spent in space. In his six trips he clocked up 803.4 days in space.

LONGEST EXTRA VEHICULAR ACTIVITY
On March 11, 2001, US astronauts Susan Helms and Jim Voss spent 8 hours 56 minutes working outside on the ISS.

OLDEST SPACE TRAVELER
On October 29, 1998, US astronaut John Glenn became the oldest space traveler ever at the age of 77. Thirty-six years earlier, in 1962, Glenn had been the first American to orbit Earth.

FIRST COMMERCIAL ASTRONAUT
On June 21, 2004, Mike Nevill became the first commercial astronaut when he piloted the first privately funded spacecraft, SpaceShipOne.

Timeline

Sputnik's outer shell protected a radio transmitter and batteries

Sputnik 1

EVER SINCE SPUTNIK went into orbit in 1957, the story of space exploration has advanced at a fast and furious pace. Below is a timeline of some of the most significant achievements. Today, we rely on satellites overhead and we take it for granted that astronauts work on a space station and that probes travel to other worlds. All this was once a dream. Who knows what the rest of the 21st century will bring?

OCTOBER 4, 1957
Sputnik 1, the world's first artificial satellite, is put into Earth orbit by the Soviet Union. The space age has begun.

Space dog Laika aboard Sputnik 2

NOVEMBER 3, 1957
The first living creature, a Soviet dog named Laika, orbits Earth in Sputnik 2.

JANUARY 2, 1959
Soviet probe Luna 1 becomes the first craft to leave Earth's gravity.

SEPTEMBER 13, 1959
Luna 2 is the first craft to land on another world when it crash-lands on the Moon.

OCTOBER 10, 1959
Soviet Luna 3 spacecraft returns the first pictures of the Moon's far side.

APRIL 12, 1961
Soviet cosmonaut Yuri Gagarin becomes the first person to travel into space.

MAY 5, 1961
Alan Shepard, traveling in Freedom 7, is the first American in space.

Yuri Gagarin

JULY 10, 1962
Telstar 1, the first realtime communications satellite, is launched by the US.

JUNE 16, 1963
Soviet cosmonaut Valentina Tereshkova becomes the first woman in space.

MARCH 18, 1965
Soviet cosmonaut Alexei Leonov makes the first space walk. He is secured to Voskhod 2 by a tether.

JULY 15, 1965
US probe Mariner 4 completes the first successful Mars flyby.

FEBRUARY 3, 1966
Soviet craft Luna 9 becomes the first to land successfully on the Moon.

DECEMBER 24, 1968
US craft Apollo 8 is the first manned craft to leave Earth's gravity and orbit the Moon.

JULY 20, 1969
The first humans walk on another world. The US astronaut Neil Armstrong is the first to walk on the Moon, Buzz Aldrin the second.

SEPTEMBER 20, 1970
Soviet probe Luna 16 lands on the Moon. It will be the first craft to collect soil and return it to Earth.

NOVEMBER 17, 1970
The first wheeled vehicle on the Moon, Soviet Lunkhod 1, starts its work.

APRIL 19, 1971
Launch of the first space station, Soviet Salyut 1.

The reflection of the photographer, Neil Armstrong, can be seen in Aldrin's visor

Buzz Aldrin walks on the Moon, 1969

DECEMBER 19, 1972
Return to Earth of Apollo 17, the sixth and last manned mission to the Moon.

DECEMBER 3, 1973
US spacecraft Pioneer 10 is the first craft to fly by the planet Jupiter after becoming the first to cross the asteroid belt.

MARCH 29, 1974
US spacecraft Mariner 10 makes the first flyby of Mercury and provides the first detailed look at the planet.

JULY 17, 1975
Apollo 18 astronauts and Soyuz 19 cosmonauts make the first US–Soviet space rendezvous.

OCTOBER 22, 1975
Soviet craft Venera 9 transmits the first images from the surface of the planet Venus.

JULY 20, 1976
The US probe Viking 1 becomes the first craft to land successfully on the planet Mars.

SEPTEMBER 1, 1979
The US probe Pioneer 11 makes the first flyby of the planet Saturn.

APRIL 12, 1981
Launch of the first reusable space vehicle, the US space shuttle, Columbia.

Columbia, the first shuttle in space

JANUARY 24, 1986
US probe Voyager 2 arrives at the planet Uranus, after making flybys of Jupiter and Saturn.

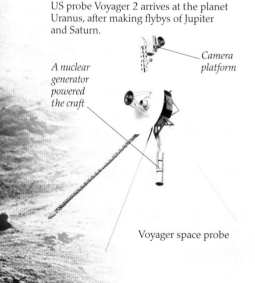

A nuclear generator powered the craft

Camera platform

Voyager space probe

The docking module for visiting craft. The station grew as new modules were added up until 1996

Space station Mir

FEBRUARY 20, 1986
The first module of the Soviet space station, Mir, is launched into orbit.

MARCH 13, 1986
Giotto, a European probe, makes the first close flyby of a comet when it approaches Halley's Comet.

AUGUST 24, 1989
Voyager 2 makes the first flyby of the planet Neptune.

APRIL 24, 1990
Launch of the Hubble Space Telescope on board the space shuttle Discovery.

OCTOBER 29, 1991
US probe Galileo makes the first flyby of an asteroid, Gaspra, before becoming the first probe to orbit the planet Jupiter (arrived 1995).

NOVEMBER 20, 1998
Zarya, the first part of the International Space Station, is launched.

NOVEMBER 2, 2000
The first crew boards the International Space Station.

FEBRUARY 12, 2001
Near Earth Asteroid Rendezvous (NEAR) becomes the first probe to land on an asteroid after orbiting Eros for one year.

JANUARY 4, 2004
A rover named Spirit arrives on Mars; 21 days later, a second rover, Opportunity, lands on the opposite side of the planet.

Kepler space telescope

JULY 1, 2004
Cassini enters orbit around Saturn and begins to study the planet and its moons.

MARCH 6, 2009
The Kepler space telescope is launched. It will look for planets that may harbor life.

The International Space Station (ISS), 2008

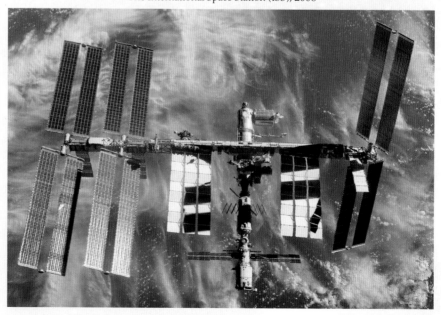

Find out more

Dramatic ADVANCES in space exploration have been echoed by innovative ways to learn about space. Books and TV were once the only source of information. Today, visitors to space centers all over the world are able to see where the action happens for themselves, share the experiences of an astronaut, do hands-on experiments in space science, and see the craft that explore space for us. Now, via the internet, anyone can access the very latest stories and pictures of space exploration.

THE EURO SPACE CENTER, TRANSINNE
These children are doing experiments in space science at the Euro Space Center at Transinne in Belgium. The Space Center covers all aspects of space exploration, but with particular emphasis on the work of the European Space Program. Exhibits include a big display on the Columbus Laboratory, the European contribution to the International Space Station. Visitors to Transinne can also try out some of the simulators used to train astronauts (pp. 22–23).

Full-scale model of the orbiter Endeavour

KENNEDY SPACE CENTER
This picture shows the Visitor Complex at NASA's huge Kennedy Space Center in Florida from where space shuttles are launched. In addition to visiting the exhibits of the Space Center (where an astronaut is available to answer questions), visitors can see the LC 39 Observation Gantry in the Space Shuttle Launch Complex and the Launch Control Center. The public can also watch space shuttle launches at the site. A Shuttle Launch Schedule and further information about this are available from the Kennedy Space Center.

MISSION CONTROL, HOUSTON, TEXAS
Space shuttles launch from Florida, but after two minutes control passes to the Mission Control Center (above) at the National Aeronautics and Space Administration's (NASA's) Johnson Space Center, in Houston, Texas. This is the center of the manned flight program where NASA astronauts are trained. Space Center Houston has a museum and offers a tour around the site to see the X-38 Assembly Building, the Shuttle Mock-up Facility, and Mission Control. During a space shuttle mission, visitors can watch activity in the Mission Control Center from a viewing gallery.

Spacecraft hang from the ceiling of the museum in Star City

STAR CITY, MOSCOW
Exhibits telling the story of the Russian manned flight program can be seen in the museum of the Yuri Gagarin Cosmonaut Training Facility at Star City, an hour from Moscow. This purpose-built town is the home and training center of Russian cosmonauts and the site of Russian Mission Control.

Other places to visit

ROSE CENTER FOR EARTH AND SPACE, AMERICAN MUSEUM OF NATURAL HISTORY, NEW YORK, NY
A space center and planetarium featuring Scales of the Universe, a 400-foot-long walkway that illustrates the vast range and size of the universe and the Hayden Planetarium, the largest virtual-reality simulator in the world.

SPACE CENTER HOUSTON, HOUSTON, TX
Visitors can see astronauts train for missions, touch a Moon rock, land a shuttle, and get a behind-the-scenes tour of NASA.

NATIONAL AIR AND SPACE MUSEUM, WASHINGTON, D.C.
The home of a large collection of original space hardware, including the Apollo 11 module, which brought back the first men from the Moon.

EXPLORING SPACE ON THE WEB

Space is an exciting topic to explore on the internet, since there is so much information available. Organizations such as the National Aeronautics and Space Administration (NASA) and the European Space Agency (ESA) have comprehensive websites full of facts and images. Below are a few subjects you may want to investigate further, and addresses of some useful websites.

THE EUROPEAN SPACE PROGRAM

News of ESA projects can be found on their homepage. The ESA launch pages give details of the next launch. Interactive features take you on a tour around the ESA Spaceport in French Guiana, South America, and show a launch sequence.

- ESA homepage: **www.esa.int**
- ESA launch pages: **www.esa.int/SPECIALS/ Launchers_Home/**

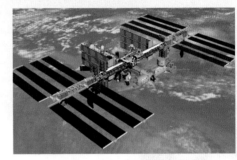

Flags from the ESA countries adorn the rocket boosters

ESA uses Ariane 5 to take payloads into space

EXPLORING SPACE

To find out more about the planets in our solar system, such as Mars (above), search on the ESA and NASA sites for details of visiting craft and future missions. For the latest images from deep space, look on the Hubble Space Telescope website.

- Hubble Space Telescope news and images: **hubblesite.org/**

THE SPACE SHUTTLE

Information on everything to do with the space shuttle, from the launch schedules and menus on board, to the position of the spacecraft (updated every hour), can be found on the NASA spaceflight website. It is also possible (with the right software) to watch live coverage of space missions online.

- NASA space shuttle information: **www.nasa.gov/mission_pages/ shuttle/main/**
- For watching space shuttle online: **spaceflight1.nasa.gov/ realdata/**

The rocket boosters are used up and discarded within two minutes of launch

The orbiter vibrates wildly as it lifts off from the launch pad

THE INTERNATIONAL SPACE STATION

For information on the International Space Station (ISS) look on the NASA spaceflight site and on the ESA's ISS pages. There are also sites that will calculate when you should be able to see the ISS from wherever you are in the world.

- For information on seeing the ISS: **spaceflight1.nasa.gov/realdata/tracking/**

ADDITIONAL WEBSITES

- NASA Kids' Club site, featuring games and activities for kids of all ages: **www.nasa.gov/audience/forkids/kidsclub/flash/**
- An amazing archive of NASA images and video clips: **www.nasaimages.org**
- Jet Propulsion Laboratory for data on space probes: **www.jpl.nasa.gov**
- Comprehensive space website with news stories: **www.space.com**
- NASM site, featuring objects from the museum: **www.nasm.si.edu**
- European Space Agency kids' site: **www.esa.int/esaKIDSen**

A Russian Soyuz TMA-13 craft carrying a crew of three approaches the International Space Station, October 2008.

Index

Acknowledgments

Dorling Kindersley would like to thank:
Heidi Graf and Birgit Schröder of the
European Space Research and Technology
Center (ESTEC), Noordwijk, the
Netherlands for their invaluable assistance;
Alain Gonfalone; Hugo Marée, Philippe
Ledent, Chantal Rolland, and Massimiliano
Piergentili of the Euro Space Center,
Transinne, Belgium (managed by CISET
International), for their cooperation and
patience; Helen Sharman; Neville Kidger;
Dr. John Zarnecki and JRC Garry of the
University of Kent, UK; MK Herbert, Ray
Merchant; Dr. David Hughes, Dr. Hugo
Alleyne, and Dr. Simon Walker of The
University of Sheffield; Prof John Parkinson
of Sheffield Hallam University; Amalgam
Modelmakers and Designers; Nicholas
Booth; JJ Thompson, Orthodontic
Appliances; Hideo Imammura of the
Shimizu Corporation, Tokyo, Japan; Dr.
Martyn Gorman of the University of
Aberdeen; Dr. Peter Reynolds; Prof Kenichi
Ijiri; Dr. Thais Russomano and Simon Evetts
of King's College London; Clive Simpson;
Karen Jefferson and Elena Mirskaya of
Dorling Kindersley, Moscow Office.

Design and editorial assistance: Darren
Troughton, Carey Scott, Nicki Waine
Additional research: Sean Stancioff
Additional photography: Geoff Brightling
Photographic assistance: Sarah Ashun
Additional modelmaking: Peter Minister,
Milton Scott-Baron
Proofreading: Sarah Owens
Index: Helen Peters
Wallchart: Peter Radcliffe, Steve Setford
Clipart CD: David Ekholm – JAlbum,
Sunita Gahir, Jo Little, Sue Malyan, Lisa
Stock, Jessamy Wood, Bulent Yusef

Picture credits:
Dorling Kindersley would like to thank:
Moscow Museum, Science Museum and
US Space and Rocket Center Alabama,
Photographs by: Stephen Oliver close up
shot 21t, James Stevenson, Bob Gathney

**The publisher would like to thank the
following for their kind permission to
reproduce their photographs:**

(Key: a-above; b-below/bottom; c-center;
f-far; l-left; r-right; t-top)

Algemeen Nederlands Persbureau: 60tl.
BOC Gases, Guildford: 52cla. **Bridgeman
Art Library:** *Adoration of the Magi*, c.1305
by Giotto, Ambrogio Bondone (c.1266-
1337) Scrovgeni (Arena) Chapel, Padua
42c. **Casio Electronics Co Ltd:** 53br. **Bruce
Coleman:** Robert P Carr 33clb. CLRC 43c.
Corbis: 52bl, 69tl, Bettmann 62bl;
Bettman-UPI 17cra, 19bl; Yuri Kotchetkov/
epa 57br; Portfolio 68-69;
Jim Sugar Photography 64bc, 65tl; Zha
Chunming/Xinhua Press 58tr. **DK Images:**
NASA 9tr, 9cra; ESTEC 36cla. **ESA
European Space Agency:** 15bl, 28bc, 29c,
31br, 34-35, 35tr, 38tr, 39cr, 42br, 43bl,
43cb, 47c, 48tl, 48bl, 49tr, 49crb, 49br, 51bl,
51tl,51br, 55tl, 60cl; AOES Medialab 54cl;
image by C.Carreau 59tr; Alain Gonfalone
37cra. **ESA:** Illustration by Medialab 55cl;
Euro Space Center, Transinne: 64tl. **Mary
Evans Picture Library:** 6tr, 6cl, 6tl, 7tl, 18tl,
20tl, 34tl. **Courtesy Garmin Ltd:**
Copyright Garmin Ltd www.garmin.com
46cl.**Genesis Space Photo Library**/CSG
1995: 10bl; 55tr. **Getty Images:** ESA/NASA
57tl, 63br; Vladimir Rys/Bongarts 46cr;
Hulton Getty 19tr, 19bc; Image Bank 53tl;
Tony Stone Images/Hilarie Kavanagh

49cr. **Dr. Martyn Gorman, University of
Aberdeen:** 48c, NASA 56tl, 54br, 55br,
64cl, 64cr. **Ronald Grant Archive:** A
Space Odyssey/MGM 58cl. **Hasbro
International Inc:** 7br. **Marc Muench:**
9br. **Matra Marconi Space UK Ltd:** 49tr.
Mattel UK Ltd: 7cb. NASA: 1, 5, 8clb,
11clb, 13tl, 14tl, 14cl, 15cla, 15br, 15tr,
18clb, 18bc, 21tr, 20-21b, 26tl, 28tr, 28clb,
28cr, 29tr, 30br, 30tl, 31cla, 31bl, 31tr, 32cl,
32bl, 32crb, 33cla, 33tl, 33tr, 35bl, 35br,
36cr, 36crb, 36clb, 36tl, 37cb, 37cl, 38cl,
44tr, 44c, 50tl, 52tr, 52bl, 56bc, 56br, 56cr,
57cr, 58bl, 59tl, 60-61 (background), 60b,
61br, 62r, 62-63 (background), 63cl, 65tr,
65cr, 66-67; Bill Ingalls 57bl; John F.
Kennedy Space Center 59bl; Johns
Hopkins University Applied Physics
Laboratory/Carnegie Institution of
Washington 54bl; John Hopkins University
Applied Physics Laboratory/Southwest
Research Institute 61tl; Johnson Space
Center 56b; JPL-Caltech 55bl; JPL-Caltech/
Ball 63cr; Pat Rawlings, SAIC 59br; NASDA
13cb; Finley Holiday Films 65b. **The
National Motor Museum, London:** 13tc.
The Natural History Museum, London:
21cla. **RIA Novosti (London):** 16bl,
17crb, 18crb, 32tr, 32bc, 33cb, 35tl, 44crb.
Professor John Parkinson/NASA: 6br,
37tl, 37tc, 37tr. **Popperfoto:** 13tr; Mark
Baker/Reuters 61tr; Mikhail Grachyev/
Reuters 19crb, 19crb, 42tl, 61bl. **Rex
Features:** 6bl, 7cl, 7tr, 34bc, 46cl. **Science
Museum/Science and Society Picture
Library:** 13ca. **Science Photo Library:**
Dr. Jeremy Burgess 8cb; Robert Chase 53c;
CNES, 1988 Distribution Spot Image 48br-
49bl; Luke Dodd 8cr; EOSAT 48tr; Victor
HabbickVisions 58cr; Johns Hopkins
University Applied Physics Laboratory
54tl; Will and Deni McIntyre 52tl; Larry
Mulvehill 53bl; NASA 9cb, 15tl, 17bl, 32c,

42tr, 50cl, 50-51, 50br, 50bl, 54cla, 60tr,
63tc, 69cr; Novosti 12tr, 17tr, 17tl, 64cl;
David Parker 48clb; Princess Margaret
Rose Orthopaedic Hospital 52cb; Roger
Ressmeyer, Starlight 10br; Scaled
Composites 59cr. **Smith Sport Optics Inc,
Idaho:** 52c. **South American Pictures:**
Tony Morrison 6cr. **Spar Aerospace
(UK) Ltd:** 11tl. **Dr. John Szelskey:** 39tl,
42cra. **Charles Thatcher:** 52br. **Times
Newspapers Ltd:** Michael Powell 38bl.
**Dean and Chapter of York, York Minster
Archives:** 7bl.

Jacket picture credits:
Front: **DK Images:** Courtesy of the Euro
Space Center, Transinne, Belgium ftr;
NASA tr; **Getty Images:** Taxi/Space
Frontiers c. *Back*: **Getty Images:** Stocktrek
RF cla (ISS); **NASA:** br, fbl; **Popperfoto:** cl.

Wallchart picture credits:
(Key: a-above; b-below/bottom; c-center;
f-far; l-left; r-right; t-top)

DK Images: Euro Space Center, Transinne,
Belgium ca (Appollo 11), NASA tl (rock),
cra (NASA badge), cra (footprint);
Courtesy of the Space & Rocket Center,
Alabama fcra (spacesuit); ESA-ESTEC crb
(Huygens illustration). **ESA:** br (Herschel).
NASA: cla (Mir), clb (ISS), fbr (Progress),
fbr (Orion). **Getty:** Bill Ingalls/NASA fbl
(launch), NASA bc (Canadarm2). **Science
Photo Library:** Ria Novosti tr (Laika).

All other images © Dorling Kindersley
For further information see:
www.dkimages.com